SMALL GAME
HUNTING

Also by TOM BRAKEFIELD

The Sportsman's Complete Book of Trophy and Meat Care
Hunting Big Game Trophies
Big Game Hunter's Digest

SMALL GAME HUNTING

Tom Brakefield

J. B. LIPPINCOTT COMPANY
Philadelphia and New York

All photographs are by the author unless otherwise indicated

U.S. Library of Congress Cataloging in Publication Data

Brakefield, Tom.
  Small game hunting.

  1. Varmint hunting—United States.
  2. Hunting—United States.   I. Title.
SK41.B7   799.2′5   78-12962
ISBN-0-397-01318-3

For JOHN SILL . . .
Editor, mentor, friend

Contents

Acknowledgments

No book, however modest or grand, is ever solely the product of one person's work. And that is certainly true in this case.

Jim Olt, Jack Jonas, Jack Atcheson, Elgin Gates and Johnny Stewart were most generous in donating photographs. Randy Phillips, a young fellow who raises crow hunting and other aspects of small game sport to a minor art form, was helpful with certain comments. Toby Tobias and Lloyd Gerhart, two of the best naturalists anywhere—self-taught or otherwise—were, as always, a help with my projects.

Johnny Stewart couldn't have been more helpful throughout. I had the pleasure of touring his game-calling manufacturing plant in Waco, Texas, and then hunting with him for over a week on a cactus-strewn, often hilarious but endlessly fascinating small game safari that stretched over most of central Texas. John can call critters with a siren song that would make Julie London flush with envy.

But there is no way this book, and most of the other good things in my life, would have come about if a whole legion of understanding small game hunters of another day hadn't taken good hunting time to help explain the "necessaries" to a wide-eyed boy who wanted, more than anything, to hunt. A lot of them are gone now, and many of the rest don't get out on the small game fields much anymore. There is no way to repay them, but I can at least acknowledge them here, and I do that with the utmost gratitude.

Introduction

Small game hunting is many things. A fine sport for outdoor buddies to share with each other and extend their all-too-short big game hunting time afield. A shared activity that adds excitement to family camping and puts some excellent (and good-for-you) meat on the table. A way for father and son or wife or daughter to get to know each other better. Or just a lazy, lovely way to spend a brisk day outdoors.

Perhaps most important of all, though, it's probably the single best way for youngsters to become acquainted with the natural world around them. Though our asphalt-bound existence is so pervasive that it at times seems to be the natural order of things, it is actually very far removed from the world that still ultimately determines our destiny. And as we stumble from one ecological near-calamity to another in this newly sensitized era, we are reminded more frequently of that fact.

Small game hunting introduces a youngster to the outdoors and to nature and teaches him or her a bit of self-reliance, responsibility and independence in the process. Not a bad set of benefits from a modest little sport that can be pursued, in a variety of forms, by almost anyone living almost anywhere in the country. Usually the cost is minimal and—best of all—*it's fun.*

Thirty years ago I knew a youngster who desperately wanted to learn how to hunt small game, and he had to do it, haltingly and ineffectually, without the benefit of parental or other direct help. A book of this sort would have been a treasure beyond compare to him. It is my earnest hope that this book will be of value to his counterparts in today's generation.

Tom Brakefield
January 1978

PART I

The Basics:
Rabbits and Squirrels

1

Cottontails on Your Own

All my life I've woods-loafed, from southern Florida's mangrove swamps to the sere steppes of Alaska's north slope, both hunting and photographing all major species of North American big game. Grizzly bear, elk, moose, mountain sheep, caribou and a host of other marvelous creatures have all been framed in my rifle sights or camera viewfinder over the years.

Occasionally, of a cold winter's night, the memories come crowding back. That's one of the joys of hunting—good hunts *never* end. I remember particularly vividly the sight of my first wild mountain ram. He was so alive and vital, standing there against the electric-blue Alberta sky and staring rather disdainfully down at us poor earthbound creatures who had to struggle so to tread but briefly the high alpine pastures he called home. Never will I forget my first way-back-in Rocky Mountain pack-string hunt that gently scoured my soul of two years' accumulated city bile.

Another magic moment was the first grizzly bear I ever stalked and shot. He crouched there on the almost sheer British Columbia mountainside, swinging his great shaggy head from side to side trying to catch my wind. I lived a year in a minute as I desperately fought to clamp down on my fatigue-jellied muscles in order to make the clean kill that he deserved.

All these thoughts and more come to mind. A very special one was the first white-tailed deer, a lad's first *big* game. But as I ponder which memory is most special of all, I am carried back to a dank, bitingly cold day when a skinny nine-year-old and his buddy, a local handyman of uncertain years, dubious repute and fine spirit, were working a spiny Tennessee hillside that seemed better for growing rocks than rabbits. Periodically the old man, a lanky "Tennessee pore" hill man dressed more in patches and holes than anything else, would stop and fortify himself against the cold with a dram from his small bottle.

The boy needed no such artificial stimulation as he eagerly pressed ahead, proudly carrying the cut-down .410 single-shot shotgun. Suddenly, from almost under the youngster's feet, a bobtailed blur exploded out and headed for the little ravine to their left. The boy and the old man, both shooting ancient single-shot hammer guns, swung through on the bunny at the same time. But the boy's gun spoke first and the rabbit folded neatly—a clean kill at thirty yards and in high gear.

The boy had taken many starlings and sparrows with his childhood BB gun, but this was his first "real" game. Though the old man offered to carry the still-warm animal in his game bag because the kid had no hunting coat, the boy would hear nothing of it. This was his kill and he would not surrender it to anyone. And he didn't. He switched it from one weary hand to the other for over an hour until he finally got smart enough to slit the rear hock with his scout knife and thread it onto his belt.

It all happened many years ago and—of course—I was that bandy-legged boy. That sparkling moment, alive and bright forever in my mind, had a profound impact. Every budding instinct that drew me toward the outdoors was crystallized and confirmed in that instant. So it has been ever since. And so it is with the majority of veteran big game hunters across the land, for the ubiquitous and prolific cottontail is far and away the most common introduction to the wonderful world of hunting and outdoor sport.

THE QUARRY

No other animal on earth is pursued or taken in numbers even beginning to approach those of the American cottontail rabbit. Of the four basic species of cottontails, and the several

More cottontail rabbits are shot for sport than any other game animal in the world, and yet these adaptable and prolific animals continue to prosper if given half a chance.

closely related types, there are in the forty-eight contiguous states probably between 60 and 100 million animals. In a peak rabbit year, probably upward of 25 million bunnies are harvested by sport hunters. All this for a rather small animal between 14 and 19 inches long and standing 6 to 7 inches at the shoulder, depending upon the subspecies and sex.

The weight of the cottontail ranges from 2 to 3½ pounds liveweight, with the females running slightly larger than the males. The basic color is brown with longer, black-tipped guard hairs giving the animal a grayer cast in winter; in summer it often assumes more of a buff or reddish tone. The underside and powder-puff tail are white. The powerful hind legs are about a foot long and muscular enough to provide both good meat for the table and a very fast starting-burst speed. (Actually, rabbits can't

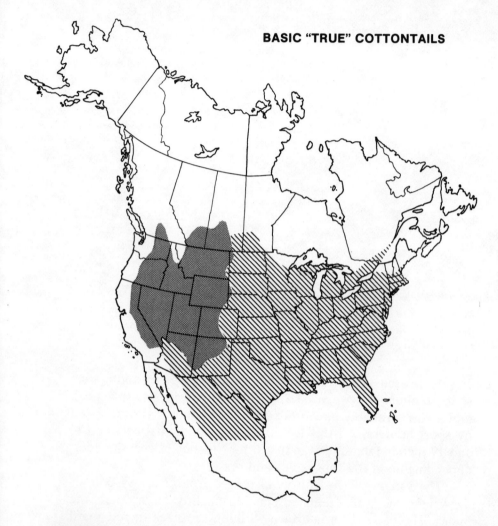

BASIC "TRUE" COTTONTAILS

 Eastern Cottontail

 Mountain or Western Cottontail

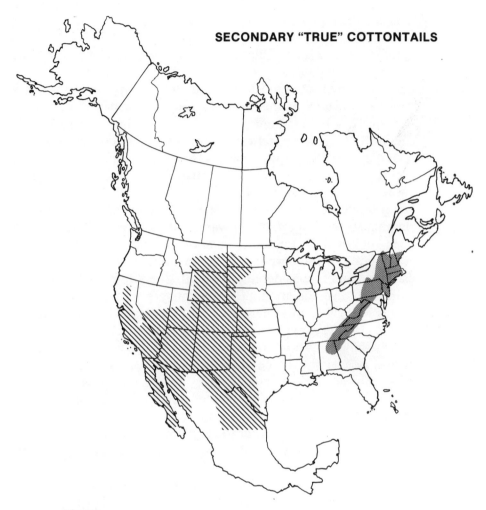

SECONDARY "TRUE" COTTONTAILS

 Desert Cottontail

 New England Cottontail

run nearly as fast as they appear to at top speed. Their leg-stretching, wildly bouncing gait makes them seem to be traveling much faster than their 18-to-22-miles-per-hour top speed, which is faster than animals such as the skunk, raccoon and opossum, but really rather slow for a mammal.)

One of the four basic "true" cottontails inhabits every one of the forty-eight contiguous states. These animals—the eastern cottontail (by far the most common and widespread of the quartet), the western or mountain cottontail, the desert cottontail and the New England cottontail—are all similar, with no significant differences in a practical hunting sense. Of four other closely related types, the pygmy rabbit is the smallest and does not have a conspicuous white tail. The brush rabbit, marsh rabbit and swamp rabbit round out the group, with the latter two always being found near water in moist bottomlands and swamps and running to the largest size. Swamp rabbits from Alabama have been recorded at 6 pounds, or about twice the size of a good cottontail. For the purposes of sport hunting, however, all these variants can be considered cottontails since they look alike and most often live and are hunted in relatively similar fashion.

A key thing to remember about mop-tails is that their fur coat is not really very efficient as animal fur goes. This single fact greatly influences how you hunt them, especially when you don't have a dog along. Since their pelage is not as waterproof or windproof as the finery sported by foxes, raccoons and other furbearers, rabbits are often obliged during the cold of winter to spend up to several hours a day washing and grooming that second-rate fur coat in order to keep it as clean, fluffy and dry as possible to maximize its efficiency. This is particularly true in the wetter sections of the country.

Rabbits simply don't like to get wet. Though they can swim well if pressed, they'd rather not. (The swamp and marsh rabbits of the Southeast are partial exceptions to this rule.) When brush and grass are heavy with dew, rain or snow, rabbits will invariably be found traveling or sitting along the wider and barer trails or roads to avoid getting wet. It's almost impossible to find one in tall, dew-soaked grass. Rabbits will usually be up and around later in the day on dewy mornings, after the sun has had time to

20

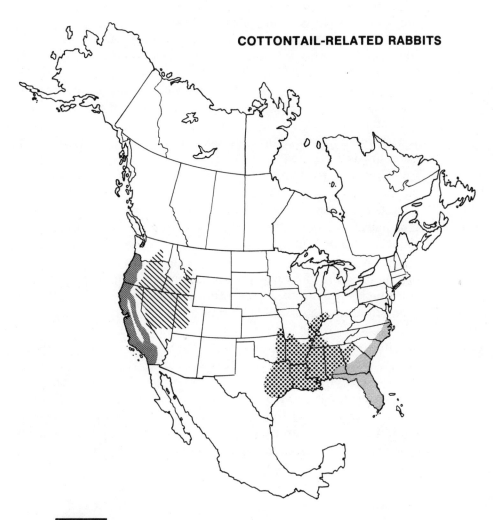

COTTONTAIL-RELATED RABBITS

 Brush Rabbit

 Pygmy Rabbit

 Swamp Rabbit ("Cane-cutter")

 Marsh Rabbit

burn most of the moisture off. They get cold so easily in that skimpy coat they have to use up a lot of energy to keep warm and a lot of time to groom and clean it. The wetter they get, the less chance they have of surviving a cold winter.

When it's snowing lightly or misting, forget about rabbit hunting. Not only will the bunnies be sitting tight somewhere and almost impossible to flush out, they'll more than likely be *under* something or *in* something in order to escape the dreaded moisture better. These "hides" can include such unlikely spots as under barns, sheds or farm outbuildings or even inside old cans or under a piece of discarded tin. Anything that will keep them dry is a possibility.

Contrary to popular belief, rabbits seldom live in or even hide in burrows, and though their long claws are good for digging, they never dig their own burrows. In dry weather cottontails generally prefer to occupy one of several outdoor "forms" that they hollow out in brush or grass, rather than seek shelter in a hole or burrow. In the form they can be alert to danger from any quarter and can escape in any direction. The burrow or hole can quickly turn into a death trap if a weasel, mink, ferret or even small house cat or terrier wanders by at the wrong time. Incidentally, these outdoor forms are located within a few hundred yards of each other, since the rabbits' total home range runs about one to two acres. Like that other supremely successful and adaptable animal, the white-tailed deer, rabbits are homebodies that survive by knowing every trail and hiding place in their domain, and they simply will not leave it unless pressed hard. Even when run by dogs, they will not stray too far from home, and this is why they run in a circle—to return to the area from which they were initially flushed.

WHEN TO HUNT RABBITS

Rabbits are most often out and around during the day when the temperatures range from about 10 to 35 degrees Fahrenheit. If it's warmer, most of their normal feeding will be at night or at least very early or very late in the day. They don't need enough additional warmth in the middle of the day to justify exposing themselves to the extra danger of feeding and moving around in full daylight.

When it's much colder than 10 degrees during the day, they'll usually lay up to conserve body energy. They have a built-in computer that tells them when they'll expend more energy stirring around in the cold and wet than they can take in by feeding. Food must be warmed by their bodies for proper digestion after they eat it, and if food is sparse, they can actually lose precious calories on that immutable calories-in/calories-out equation that ultimately determines whether they will survive the rigors of winter. A rabbit in good condition will usually fast for a week or longer if necessary, rather than squander energy by getting wet and wind chilled as it stirs around looking for food.

In addition to temperature, two other factors determine when and where to look for rabbits: moisture and wind chill. When the wind has a cutting edge to it, look for them to be hiding in gullies, ravines or at least in forms with some sort of windbreak. If the sun is out, they may be found on the sunny southern exposures of the hills and draws even if the weather is fairly raw. That extra bit of warmth helps considerably. If it's an overcast, blustery day with a moisture-laden atmosphere that chills, rabbits may seek out a hole or burrow even though the temperature reading may be only a few degrees below that of the moderately sunny, dry and non-windy day on which they'd be perfectly comfortable outside. Always check the southern exposures of draws and cuts for rabbits or their tracks during sunny but cold days.

HOW TO HUNT RABBITS WITHOUT A DOG

The first thing you should do to hunt rabbits on your own is learn as much about your quarry as you can. Natural history books will tell you what they eat (basically, anything that is green, though they do have some preferences such as garden vegetables like lettuce and celery), where they live and how they live. Then learn about the areas you want to hunt. Walk them

Billy Bibb, Alabama rabbit hunter supreme, shows the difference in size between a "standard" cottontail and its much larger near relative, the swamp rabbit (right).

over thoroughly at different times of year to see how they look during the "bare" season of winter and the overgrown seasons of spring and summer. Note all chuckholes, burrows and other holes that may harbor rabbits during bitter cold weather or when pushed hard by dogs.

Keep up with the places where you successfully flushed rabbits in the past. Whenever a rabbit is killed in a prime territory, another one seems to appear almost immediately. The best place to find rabbits is where you have had good luck finding

24

them in the past. Billy Bibb, the best rabbit hunter I ever knew, used to keep detailed records about where he jumped rabbits. Not only did he merely indicate the spot, he also recorded the date, time of day and prevailing weather and wind conditions. A veteran rabbit hunter who killed over twenty thousand in a long hunting career, Billy was shrewd enough to know that his "rabbit bible" was the key not only to some fond memories but also to continued good hunting.

This learning-the-game-field approach simply cannot be overemphasized. It's amazing how many veteran big game hunters will approach larger animals in a methodical, organized fashion by first learning all they can about the quarry and by scouting the area to be hunted thoroughly, both before and during the hunting season, to learn where the feeding and bedding areas are and where the trails are—and yet many of these same sportsmen approach small game hunting in the most haphazard fashion imaginable, just selecting an area to be hunted at random and then kicking their way through the brushy spots that are potential cover in order to try to flush out a rabbit. They wouldn't get many deer by hunting that way, and more often than not they don't get too many rabbits, either.

Rabbits are biological creatures with certain physical requirements and preferences just as deer, elk or bear are. True, their "game field" is a mini-sized patch of a couple of acres, but the same basics hold true. They have preferred bedding areas that vary according to weather conditions. They have favorite feeding and watering spots, and there are certain trails and crossings that they continue to use. Learning about these spots by capitalizing on the knowledge gained from past hunts or from just tramping around in the woods in the off-season not only makes you a more productive rabbit hunter but makes the whole sport more meaningful and more fun. And what better way to introduce youngsters to the rhythm and logic of the natural world? Youngsters respond to something logical and understandable. And that's just what this approach to small game hunting is. It's the mystifying, haphazard approach to "kicking out rabbits" that makes youngsters bored and restless in an amazingly short time.

Thick southern river bottoms are ideal habitat for varying combinations of the marsh rabbit, the swamp rabbit, and the basic or "standard" cottontail rabbit.

After learning as much as you can about the quarry, scouting the area to be hunted and keeping up with past hunting experiences to apply them to future hunts, it's time to begin to apply all this. And what fun that is!

On cold sunny days, the habit rabbits have of sitting out in their forms provides some very sporty hunting for the hunter without a dog—especially if there is tracking snow on the ground. The hunter can check sunny areas for bunnies trying to soak up the warmth, or follow tracks, and ease up on the animals as they lie in their forms. Sometimes the rabbit can be spotted from a long distance away, especially against the snow. Binoculars, a lightweight and low-power model, can be especially handy

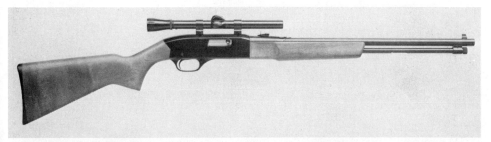

When hunting cottontails without a dog, especially in a light "tracking snow," a scope-sighted .22 rifle such as this model 190 semi-automatic rimfire can provide ideal sport—and be an effective game getter! (Photo courtesy of WINCHESTER-WESTERN)

here. When moving along, glass those far "rolls" or folds in the land at the edge of fields or along tree lines just as if you were spotting for big game. The principle is exactly the same in this type of hunting.

Either a shotgun or a rifle can be used. The rifle is more sporting and more fun if you are hunting an area thick enough with rabbits and offering enough snow or open conditions to ensure some spotting at longer distances. Then you can either shoot the sitting rabbit long distance or, even more fun, circle around if necessary and attempt to flush the bunny out in fairly open going so that you have an opportunity for a decent running shot. It's tough to hit a running cottontail with a .22 rifle, and I readily confess that I miss far more than I hit, even under the best of conditions. But there's a feeling of supreme satisfaction when you do make a clean kill on a zigzagging bunny with a rifle, and even near misses are excellent marksmanship practice for deer season. A fast-firing autoloader or "automatic," as they are called by some, is the best rifle for this brand of sport.

If you know where the rabbit is before it flushes, and if you have some idea where it'll run, you'll find yourself hitting more of these running shots than you would expect—especially if you approach them properly. Cottontails, like white-tailed deer and unlike the long-legged jackrabbit, are hiders rather than runners. They'd rather fold those ears back and sit tight if at all possible. Thus, if you approach a rabbit reasonably slowly and in a some-

27

Today's man-wise, "civilized" farmland cottontails will often sit tight until you almost step on them before flushing.

what random, zigzag fashion, without ever looking or pointing directly at it, many times you can get very close. I have almost caught them with my bare hands doing so.

The trick is to keep the rabbit guessing. As long as he thinks you haven't seen him and he has those long ears laid back, you can just about step on him. (How many times have you practically stumbled over them accidentally!) Watch those ears. Once they begin to twitch and stand up, get ready to shoot, because the rabbit's just decided that the jig is up and he'd be healthier taking the sun somewhere else.

When hunting with a dog, you will obviously be working into the wind, or upwind, most times, since the dogs are following the wind-borne scent. Even when working without a dog, however, it's usually a good idea to hunt into the wind rather than downwind, with the wind behind you. Rabbits invariably sit facing into the wind when resting in their form. They do this for several reasons. Facing into the wind means that the scent of

28

danger can be better picked up. But even the most casual observer can note that those big bunny ears imply a keen sense of hearing. Facing into the wind means that sounds are also better broadcast to them. Yes, the rabbit can and does swivel those big ears almost all the way around to catch sounds from other quarters, but undoubtedly holding its ears in that position for a long period of time takes some energy. Like the rest of us, a rabbit would just as soon do things the easy way and face into the breeze.

Also, that second-rate fur coat mentioned earlier is a somewhat more efficient insulator and is warmer if the rabbit is facing into the wind and the wind is blowing with the grain of the hair rather than up under and thus penetrating to the body. So your chances of walking up on a rabbit and surprising it are generally much better if you're hunting upwind and thus coming up from behind (since the rabbit is also facing upwind most of the time). At least that's the case on cold, clear and sunny winter days. On damp, overcast days, hunting into the wind doesn't matter so much because rabbits will tend to be "inside" under something, or at least be much better hidden, and you'll have a tough time spotting them before they spot you. These are the days to take the shotgun rather than the rifle for those sudden running shots.

Kicking rabbits out of thick cover without a dog is tough—especially if you're after the new breed of cagey backyard or farmyard rabbit that is used to seeing and being around people and doesn't spook easily. The best approach is to be out extremely early or late in the day. Rabbits, like most other animals, have become far more nocturnal than many people realize. If it has been a moonlit night, chances are they may have fed some during the night (if it wasn't too cold to be out). If it was a dark night or a very cold night, however, early and late in the day may be the best time to catch them out and around. Some of the mouth-blown or hand-held noisemakers (the ones driven by compressed air that really shriek out the decibels) can be a big aid in helping to roust rabbits out of their hiding places. (Be sure to check your state hunting regulations to make sure this is legal.)

Incidentally, don't forget to check the junk piles. These can

Discarded man-made heavy implements such as automobiles, farm machinery, or, in this case, old coal-mining equipment, often make a better refuge than natural cover. And the rabbits know it! Always check sites like this out, and you'll usually find good hunting.

be veritable gold mines. Though it is tough to get rabbits out of the larger ones without the aid of a dog (we'll cover junk-pile hunting more thoroughly in the next chapter, about rabbit hunting with dogs), there is often a single rabbit hiding in some of the smaller refuse areas that hardly even qualify for the title "pile." I have kicked rabbits out of postage-stamp-size areas of junk consisting of only two or three tin cans and maybe a flat sheet of corrugated tin or a few odd sticks of lumber. Whenever all this can be turned over by hand, you can force the rabbit out, unless there are holes underneath that it can sneak into. Incidentally, some of the cannier rabbit hunters check these small junk areas on every hunt, and if they spot a hole they fill it in or cover it up so that if the refuse lures a rabbit into residence later there won't be a built-in storm cellar to flee into. And, of course, the rabbit won't dig another once you have filled in the existing one adequately.

HOW TO IMPROVE YOUR RABBIT HUNTING

There are some simple, easy things you can do to improve the rabbit hunting on your own land or that of a friend or acquaintance, if you have permission to do so. Though cottontails are still quite plentiful in most areas, the old lament that "there just aren't as many as there used to be!" is all too true.

The enormous bags collected around the turn of the century when a hunter could often shoot twenty, thirty or even more rabbits in an afternoon are no longer possible. The decline has had little or nothing to do with sport hunting. Rabbits suffer from an 85-percent mortality rate annually, whether they are hunted or not. The problem is compounded by a vastly increased human population, which has, in turn, a greatly increased standard of living. The support of these additional millions at a higher physical and economic standard requires more intensive land use, which means less ground left fallow and overgrown for wildlife populations. Not only is more land being farmed, but it is being farmed on a far "cleaner" basis, which means fewer hedgerows, overgrown fence lines, odd pockets of brush and bramble or small groves of trees for wildlife to find shelter in. There is plenty of food for wildlife, but it has been proven over and over again that shelter is more critical for high wildlife densities than even food or water.

Even today, however, almost every farm or field will have small pockets or mini-areas that aren't suitable for cultivation. Don't keep them mowed clean and don't remove or burn the brush. In fact, take brush gathered from other areas being cleared for cultivation and deposit it in these small nonfarming spots. Stack the brush tightly, with the larger pieces on the bottom to keep the piles from collapsing and shifting so much, and leave it in these spots as cover and homes for rabbits. Wiring larger brush piles together helps keep them from dispersing and being blown and washed away.

Another good trick is to cut any evergreen trees growing in these spots about halfway through and lay the crown on the ground. (If necessary, transplant some evergreens to these areas, let them get established, and then follow through by cutting them as I am outlining here.) If this is done properly, the tree will continue to live for a considerable period of time, thus ensuring that this "living" brush pile doesn't decompose as fast as a dead one would. You don't need large trees. Eight-foot or ten-foot-high trees will do fine, and you don't need many of them—just a few spotted at strategic spots. You'll be amazed at the difference they'll make in your rabbit-hunting action.

It's been estimated that a single pair of cottontails could, with their offspring, produce up to 350,000 rabbits in a five-year period. They breed like . . . rabbits, remember? So the problem with rabbits isn't fecundity or food, it's cover. All you need do to increase their survival rate is improve their cover and your sport will pick up immediately (literally the same year) and dramatically.

Another simple thing that could greatly improve rabbit hunting would be an earlier opening of the rabbit hunting season. All too many fish and game departments wait until October or November. As mentioned before, it's been conclusively proven that rabbits, through normal depredations such as other preddators, disease and highway accidents, suffer an annual mortality rate of 85 percent whether they are hunted by man or not. Rabbits breed as early as the age of nine months, and they have a minimum of two to three litters per year, with reproduction being year-round in the more southerly, warm-weather states. If adequate cover and food exist, it's extremely difficult if not downright impossible to shoot them out by sport hunting.

In August of each year, the rabbit population peaks, with bumper crops of summer bunnies beginning to reach maturity. By the time the November hunting season opens in many eastern states, there has been a 50- to 60-percent mortality rate even without hunting. An enormous portion of this is predation by the automobile, which benefits mostly the vultures and crows.

32

Year-round and nationwide, it's a pretty safe bet that man kills more rabbits with his automobiles than with his guns. Those millions of rabbits could be harvested by sportsmen rather than by drivers if the season were opened earlier.

OUTLOOK FOR RABBITS AND RABBIT HUNTING

The outlook for rabbit hunting is good. Rabbits are, again like white-tailed deer, a successional species that basically responds well to man and his land clearing and crop growing (as long as he doesn't clear *all* the cover off the land). Rabbits are adaptable, fecund animals which, if given any chance at all, will do well in today's and tomorrow's world, continuing to furnish more sport for more hunters than any other species of animal.

Like any other birds or animals, rabbits are inherently interesting—just as marvelous and unique a creation in their own right as the bighorn sheep or the grizzly bear. There are no "dull" animals, only dull minds and uncomprehending eyes seeing them. Rabbits furnish more sport and probably more meat than any other game animal in the world. That's quite an accolade for an unassuming little animal that usually weighs only a couple of pounds.

2

Rabbit Hunting with a Dog

The morning sun had already turned from cool amber to hot yellow as Gerry Ashberry and I locked the pickup and made ready. That meant we were running two hours late already.

While we loaded our guns, the fall wind freshened and chilled with the promise of colder winter weather to come. We had two beagles with us, Gerry's four-year-old named Barney and my green, largely untrained year-old pup, Radar. Both yipped enthusiastically and lightened themselves several times, as excited hunting dogs that know they are about to hunt have been doing from time immemorial.

We started off across a large stubble field that was seemingly as open and flat as a chessboard, except for the thin five-o'clock shadow of the stubble itself. At the other end, a heavy fencerow (which is, alas, a rarity in these days of "clean" farming) beckoned, and beyond it lay a thick weed lot leading up to some scattered groves of hardwoods bordered with some dandy brush piles where undergrowth had been cleared out and stacked. Ideal rabbit country.

One would expect even a field mouse to be readily visible anywhere in the stubble we were crossing. Certainly no self-respecting rabbit would be out so late in the morning in this kind of open terrain. Gerry and I hadn't even really started hunting as we strode carelessly along, paying little attention to what was going on as we chatted together.

Radar frisked and frolicked along as any glad-to-be-alive young pup will do. But Barney, a veteran of many hunts, was already running a nose-to-the-ground pattern on something up ahead. Hardly two hundred feet from the truck and twenty-five feet from us, Barney's tail suddenly went electric as he bellowed and shifted into stubby-legged overdrive. Barely five feet from *him*, a fat Pennsylvania cottontail magically erupted from the "empty" ground and streaked for the safety of the fencerow.

Beagles and other rabbit dogs are seldom ever able to run down a healthy rabbit and catch it outright. The few times I have seen this happen have either involved rabbits weakened by an especially severe winter or, rarer still, a situation where the dogs were able to run the bunny over flat, bare ground for forty-five minutes or longer and the rabbit wasn't able to put its faster-turning "scatback" abilities to work to tire and confuse the dogs.

The particular old mop-tail that electrified Barney had hung tough until we almost stepped on him, so that he literally squirted out from between our feet when flushed (not unusual with today's man-wise farm-bred cottontails). In doing so he almost outsmarted himself as he barely had a two-jump head start on the dogs and they had shifted into high gear almost as fast as the rabbit. Barney was pressing him hard, nipping right at the seat of his pants, while Radar followed a scant six feet behind.

Gerry and I stared goggle-eyed at the unexpected game for a second and then swung our guns through onto the scampering target, but we held our fire. Barney was simply too close, and in any rabbit hunting with a dog, the dog's safety is always the first priority. If in doubt, the hunter should let the rabbit go without firing. Chances are the dog will run the bunny back by the waiting hunter on the next round, since rabbits almost always tend to circle around when chased by a dog.

As we hesitated there with our guns tracking the madly jinking and jittering rabbit, he suddenly cut sharply to the left and turned on the afterburner, leaving Barney momentarily behind. My shiny new shotgun barked once, and the bunny, dusted along by a load of number 6 shot, came to a nose-skidding stop against a big hunk of stubble in the winter-bare field.

Pocketing the rabbit after the dogs had worried with him a bit, I remarked to Gerry, "You know, if Barney hadn't been here

35

Though not a fast runner, a cottontail can outturn a dog every time, and they are seldom caught by even the fastest of rabbit hounds unless they are unhealthy to begin with.

to keep him honest, we never would have known that rabbit was in the same county."

"Not even if we had walked right over him," Gerry agreed.

So productivity is just one reason that using a good rabbit dog is probably the best way to hunt the wily cottontail. Another reason is that having a good dog along makes the hunting twice as exciting and more fun. There's just more sheer *sport* to watching a beagle or other good rabbit dog bounce up a rabbit and yodel it around the countryside and back your way for a good shot. Best of all, hunting rabbits with a dog is so easy if it's done properly. Choosing a dog, developing and keeping him, and hunting with him are all easy, straightforward items requiring no special training or aptitude on the part of the hunter and dog owner.

THE "BEST" RABBIT DOG

"Best" is a dangerous word to use. Hunting dogs are all special to their owners, and some sportsmen just plain prefer

36

one type over another. Also, the breed that works best for you can vary a good bit, depending on where you live, what type of terrain and cover you will be hunting rabbits in and how thickly populated with rabbits your area is. I've hunted cottontails with everything from basset hounds, overage coonhounds and fox-hounds, and failed bird dogs to mutts of dubious ancestry who would defy description, and I've found that most all of them can do a passable to good job in the right circumstances if you know a bit about what you're doing.

Basset Hounds

If you live in an area of fairly open cover where the rabbits aren't too thickly populated (which is usually the case in such areas), a basset hound might be a good choice. Bassets, along with bloodhounds, have the best noses in dogdom. If rabbits are few and far between, a basset is about the best dog to locate an old scent and stay with it until the bunny is finally located. Though only standing 14 inches at the shoulder, bassets are compact heavyweights scaling 45 to 60 pounds. They are short-coated animals that thrive well in warmer to moderate-winter areas, and they do well as house dogs or semi-house dogs because of their good tempers, short coats and the fact that everyone likes a basset. If your dog must double as a suburban or exurban pet, you might consider a basset. They don't need a really large area for exercise and maintenance.

Two other good points about bassets are that they are rather slow and they are close-ranging dogs. Their slowness is good because a rabbit pressed too hard too quickly will tend to dive down a hole and thus end the race and the sport. And the basset's close-ranging tendencies make this dog easier to control and keep up with, especially if any of the hunters are youngsters, oldsters or people with a health problem. A long-legged bird dog or full-sized hound that has been converted into a rabbit dog can be very tiring to hunt behind.

On the negative side, bassets are a bit larger than some other rabbit breeds and thus take a bit more feed to maintain and a bit more room to keep. The latter can be an important point if they are to be squeezed into a smaller, bungalow-type suburban home already well staffed with youngsters.

37

Terriers

Fox terriers, so-called "rat terriers" and various crossbreeds among the smaller terrier types can make very good rabbit runners indeed—especially if much hunting is in thick cover or in the inevitable junk piles that seem to proliferate around the edges of today's exurban farmlands. Rat terriers are small dogs with short coats that stand only about 9 to 11 inches at the shoulder and weigh some 5 to 8 pounds when fully grown. This makes them considerably smaller and more lightly built than the standard 13-inch beagle, which will weigh in at a considerably chunkier (and wider-bodied) 18 to 25 pounds. Though this "rat terrier" breed is not recognized by the American Kennel Club, these dogs have been around for many years and certainly breed true.

This selfsame little dog, always referred to as a "rat terrier," was much in evidence around the farming communities of Alabama and Tennessee where I grew up, and I see rat terriers all the time around farming areas in Pennsylvania. They are sharp-faced, alert-eyed little dogs, and though their coats may vary considerably from smooth-haired to wiry and their colors run from black-on-white to liver-on-white, they are invariably keen and aggressive hunters. These little fellows are pint-sized terrors, and they put any cat to shame as an aggressive and deadly ratter. I once saw two of them kill over fifty large and vicious norway rats in a single morning while their farmer-owners used them to police an old rat-infested granary.

Many believe that this little dog is basically a toy version of the classic fox terrier. In any event, these terriers can negotiate places almost as tight as rabbits themselves, and they can be used to flush rabbits out of extremely thick natural cover or junk piles where even a beagle would be too big. They are also an ideal choice if the rabbit-hunting dog must double as a family pet in suburbia. Because of their small size, their upkeep is negligible, and they usually cost only $25 to $50 when purchased from people who breed them. To top it off, they are almost always as good-natured as beagles or bassets!

However, these little terriers are far better at digging a rabbit out of extremely thick cover, man-made or natural, for a single fleeting shot at the point of flush than they are at running a rabbit around past the hunter in the classic beagle-and-bunny fashion. Their legs are so short and they are so tiny (their very advantages in the thickets and tangled piles of junk) that they can't run well in snow over one or two inches deep or through tall grass or weeds. Though lionhearted, they are simply too small for this heavier-duty running and tire quickly. But if you must literally dig your bunnies out of tight cover and then course them over relatively open cultivated fields, the little rat terrier is the ideal dog for you.

Beagles

The best dog for the most rabbit hunters is undoubtedly the beagle. Along with bloodhounds and otter hounds, they are the oldest of all hound breeds and throughout their many centuries of existence have been bred for one purpose and one purpose only—to run hares and rabbits. They have good size and stamina and are fast enough but not too fast. They usually possess a good voice and thus are easy to keep up with and a joy to listen to when in hot pursuit of the quarry. They have a good nose but are not so keen-nosed (like the basset) that they will strike an old trail and spend too much time trying to unravel it while many fresher, hotter trails abound. Able to negotiate heavy cover and moderately deep snow well, they have the stamina and heart to hunt avidly all day long and tend to be a healthy, even-tempered and intelligent pet.

Beagles are now the third highest in registrations among the hundred-plus breeds recognized by the American Kennel Club (outranked only by the nonhunting French poodle and German shepherd). As a dog that must pull double duty as an inexpensive family pet and hunting dog, live within the confines of a suburban lot, and be called upon to hunt under a wide variety of terrain and weather conditions, this tidy-coated mini-hound is a tough act for any other rabbit dog to match!

CHOOSING YOUR RABBIT DOG

Should I Buy a Male or a Female? The most important differences occur from dog to dog as individuals and not between

A good pack of beagles means much more than a fuller game bag. Dogs make the whole sport of rabbit hunting twice as much fun and twice as exciting, because they enjoy the hunt at least as much as humans do.

This hunter is calling his beagles in by blowing on a homemade cow horn that he has trained them to respond to. This helps bring the dogs in quickly when a pack of several are being hunted in heavy cover and may be out of sight or shouting distance.

sexes. Some dogs are just more alert and better-natured than others. If I did have to choose by sex only, however, I would say that females tend to hunt just as readily as males, are more alert and fight less when they run with strange dogs.

Unless I have definite plans to breed the dog for pups, I usually have either the male or the female "fixed" by the vet. The operation is easy and painless and usually, on rabbit-sized dogs, only costs around $25 to $35. A spayed female or "doctored" male dog is far more loyal, easier to manage and easier to bring in from the hunt. There are no troubles with the other local dogs around the house when the breeding season comes, and there are far too many feral dogs running loose simply because thoughtless owners neglected to have them cut or penned up when the female dogs came into season. Though neutered dogs are supposed to become rather stolid and lose liveliness and

41

intelligence, I have found this to be within acceptable limits, especially in the case of dogs that continue to receive a reasonable amount of personal attention after the operation.

Which Is Better, a Larger or a Smaller Dog? Beagles come in two sizes or "standards": those below 13 inches in shoulder height and those between 13 and 15 inches in shoulder height. Both are good rabbit dogs, but since many rabbit-hunting areas seem to be comprised of smaller and smaller fields in crowded suburban and exurban areas, I've noticed more and more suburban hunters opting for the smaller dog.

Is a Registered, or Purebred, Dog Better? Not at all. In fact, many veteran rabbit hunters are definitely biased against pedigreed or purebred dogs. I would make sure that the dog is *predominantly* beagle, terrier or basset, or whatever breed you've selected as being best for you, but there is no problem at all with having a mixed-breed dog under those conditions. And the mixed breeds are almost always far cheaper (often free!) than the registered dogs.

Where Is the Best Place to Buy a Good Rabbit Dog? Since the best place to buy a good rabbit dog can vary from area to area, the first thing you should do is locate some local veteran rabbit hunters (through a nearby sporting-goods store, sportsman's club or newspaper outdoor columnist) and find out where they get their dogs. They may even have some pups for sale at a reasonable price. Other possibilities are checking the local newspaper classified ads or tabloid "shopper's guides" or calling local kennels. The kennel dogs will be pedigreed and thus more expensive in most cases.

It's usually not a good idea to buy hunting dogs from pet stores. Too many pet stores have outrageously high prices, the bloodlines of their stock are often suspect, and the care given their "inventory" is of questionable quality. It is common practice for some pet stores to buy cheap dogs from local backyard breeders (who often don't care for their dogs well) and then turn around and raise the price four to ten times after giving the dogs a hasty bath.

42

How Much Should I Pay? There's no pat answer to this one. Dogs tend to cost more in the North and the East than in the Midwest or the South. Pedigreed dogs cost more than crossbreeds. Pedigreed bassets are likely to be more expensive than pedigreed beagles, and both will probably be a bit more than what is claimed to be a "pedigreed" rat terrier. Some of the good crossbreeds may be had for nothing or for a nominal cost of $10 to $25. The terriers may run $50 to $100 and the beagles often run upward of $100 and more. Don't forget that you should budget a few dollars extra to have your new dog thoroughly examined by a vet, wormed and inoculated against all the basic canine horrors. Never accept the unsubstantiated word of the seller that the dog has been wormed and received all necessary shots. If you don't have a notarized paper from a vet to that effect, don't take any chances with your new hunting pal. Put him through the basic health routine again.

SEVEN GENERAL RULES FOR
DEVELOPING ANY RABBIT DOG

1. *Start them out at the right age.* I wouldn't try to hunt a rabbit dog seriously before he's about six months old. He's usually not sure enough of himself physically and, like most other youngsters of any species, he's still too addle-headed and with too short an attention span for serious work. Even at six months I'd watch him closely—especially if he isn't running with his mother or other dogs that he knows and feels comfortable with. If he is too timid and scared and isn't getting into the spirit of the hunt after you've been out for about an hour, I'd break it off and bring him in. No sense working him too hard too soon to convert what should be the joy of his life (the hunt) into a nightmare for him just because you are a bit impatient. Dogs develop both rapidly and individually during this adolescent stage, and if he wasn't ready at six months, he should be at eight or nine.

2. *Run him with older dogs to begin with.* Rabbit rousting with a dog is among the simplest and most straightforward of

field sports, far different from the more complex dog sports related to upland bird or duck hunting. Most dogs would rather chase rabbits than anything else, and all the basic rabbit breeds like beagles already have the right instincts bred into them. A lot of formal training just isn't necessary.

Let the beginning dog run with older dogs to get the idea of what is expected of him. His mother is best of all. He knows and trusts her. If that's not possible, try to let him get acquainted with any strange dogs *before* he actually works with them in the field. If they don't scare him too much during the hunt, he'll catch onto things pretty fast.

3. *Don't give up too soon.* Dogs, like people, develop in stages and at variable rates. Some "teenagers" are much more mature than others. If your dog seems a bit slow to pick up the game, don't despair. Keep trying. Remember, this is what he's been bred for (if he's a beagle, basset or rat terrier) over the years. All you have to do is help him tap the natural instincts that are already there.

Also, don't become unduly discouraged if your dog seems to regress a bit periodically. Depending upon how often you hunt him, he really shouldn't smooth out and hit his full competence until he's about two years old, and chances are he'll not be at his peak performance until he's three.

I'll never forget one rabbit hunt we made a couple of seasons ago. Our bag wasn't exceptional, nor was anything else about that day except for one thing. On a four-gun three-dog hunt, Robbie Tobias's little beagle bitch bounced up—all by herself—seven of the nine rabbits we kicked out. It was her first full season of working with a patient and understanding master and she was responding marvelously, making up for some of her rough edges with an eagerness and joy to hunt that would delight any hunter–dog owner's heart.

This two-year-old dog had been given to Robbie several months earlier by a high-pressure type who assured him that she was "no good as a hunting dog" because he had been "trying to hunt her since before she was six months old." The thin, nervous little "black" beagle sure didn't look like much of a prize at that stage of the game, shivering and whining whenever anyone looked her way.

Robbbie took his time and worked with the dog gently, gradually winning her confidence. Then he introduced her to—and let her become familiar with—the other dogs she would run with during the killing season, one at a time. There was no fear or unfamiliarity among the dogs by the time the season opened, and the little hound took to chasing cotton like the natural hunter she had been all along.

Obviously, the dog's first master had tried to force her to hunt too young and then had compounded his mistake by being too impatient for results. Then he gave up on her too soon. Though Robbie was low gun on that hunting day, I'm sure he will remember that particular hunt as one of his most rewarding!

4. *Treat your dog evenhandedly.* The more I'm around beagles and other four-legged rabbit types, the more I think they resemble kids in many ways. You can spoil a dog and ruin it for hunting in the process. That doesn't mean that "house" beagles don't make good hunting dogs. Quite the contrary. I think that a good house dog—if handled firmly and fairly—has many advantages over a kennel-reared dog because of the extra attention (and, thus, development) received.

Incidentally, Billy Bibb, the most accomplished rabbit-hound man I know of anywhere in the country, agrees with me on this point. Though he usually keeps a pack of between ten and fourteen running beagles (he's *serious* about his sport!), he purposefully rotates his young pups so that they each spend some time in the house with him and his family as they're growing up. Billy feels this gives the dogs a chance to get to know him better, and he gets a better idea of their capabilities and how fast they are maturing so he knows when to start them hunting and how fast to bring them along. Also, the attention the dog picks up along the way helps to accelerate its development—that is, if that attention isn't too undisciplined and slipshod.

The young pup must be treated patiently but with firm discipline, both at home and in the field. For instance, when you take a young dog out in the field and he whines because he doesn't want to cross water or a solid obstruction of some sort, *don't help him over.* He'll tend to expect help from then on and you will keep him from mastering these challenges on his own. Be patient and let him work it out for himself. If he can't, he's still too young to be afield for serious hunting.

At home, although it's fine to supplement a dog's food with nonfat-meat table scraps (and a bit of fat is fine during a cold winter if the dog is exercising a good bit outdoors), never hand-feed your dog directly from the table. That's one of the quickest ways to destroy discipline. Our dog knows if he doesn't get it out of the dog bowl, he's not going to get it at all. Annoying whining and begging around the table are more a sign of a bad dog owner than they are of a bad dog!

5. *Work your dog some in the off-season if your state allows.* Check your state hunting regulations to see if you can run rabbits out of hunting season. If so, it's both a good idea and a lot of fun. This year-round running keeps the dog in trim both physically and mentally—and he'll love it. The fact that you're not shooting the rabbits he jumps won't hurt anything, or at least it never has with me. Apparently the chase itself is enough for most beagles (as long as you do kill some of the rabbits during the season), and there doesn't seem to be a negative effect as is often the case when you don't shoot birds over a good bird dog.

If you live in a hot-weather state and want to hunt during the summer, try running your dog in the evening or at night (again, if your state law allows). This will keep the footpads hard and the muscle tone up without putting the animal through that get-in-shape crunch that can occur so suddenly and painfully at the beginning of hunting season each year and can actually kill an older, out-of-condition dog. Besides being good toners, you'll find these off-season rambles to be a lot of fun, especially if shared with some buddies and their dogs, and they help make your sport a year-round affair.

6. *Keep your dog fit and trim during hunting season.* The average beagle-and-bunny race varies considerably in both length of distance covered and time spent running, depending

upon the steepness and variety of terrain, the amount of cover, the kind of weather and wind conditions and various other factors. Most rabbit races are shorter than they seem, however. I once clocked several and found that they averaged less than ten minutes apiece in that particular area. Even so, they're a real workout for a dog, especially one that has gotten flabby in the off-season and is over six years old.

If your dog hasn't been running much in the off-season, start gradually before the season opens, so that you can harden up his footpads. Otherwise he'll tend to overdo things when the season opens and may wear his pads right off, especially if you're running him in rocky country. That's painful, and it cuts into your precious hunting time while he is recovering. It could even leave him out for most of a short season. Be sure to keep his toenails clipped short enough so that they barely make an impression in a muddy track, if they aren't already worn down to that length from the dog's normal running activities.

Of course, you'll want to feed your dog several hours before a strenuous hunt and then take the food away. Although the arguments never cease about whether to feed them "wet" or "dry" before a hunt, I do it both ways, depending upon how hot it is and how long we'll be hunting ("wet" for hotter, shorter hunts and "dry" for cooler, longer hunts).

Remember, dogs are subject to heart attacks, strokes and the other nefarious ailments that strike out-of-condition human hunters when we overexert. I once knew of a prized hound that was ordered through the mail with a 50-percent down payment approaching $1,000. He arrived safe and in good condition and was nurtured and coddled like venetian glass. When the season finally came, the fat and flabby two-year-old promptly had a heart attack and died after the first long, strenuous hunt. With the sadder but wiser owner still owing $950 on him! So keep your dog toned up or don't hunt him too hard and long until he is in good condition.

7. *Don't feed him the lights!* I let my dog worry the dead rabbit a bit on a fresh kill, especially the first rabbit or two of the hunt. That's enough to keep him lively and full of the hunt. I

never let him eat the rabbit's entrails, even though I usually dress the game afield shortly after killing it. The dog could pick up tapeworm or other pesky parasites from the uncooked liver or intestines.

JUNK PILE HUNTING

I once wrote a magazine piece called "Jackpot in the Junk Piles" that caused quite a bit of reader comment, and in this era of rapid urbanization I would be remiss if I didn't sketch in some of the same information in a book of this nature.

One of the changing land-use patterns in the last twenty years or so has been the demise of the small family farms in many of the exurban belts that mark the transition areas between the suburbs and the true "country" around our major cities. Although some of these plots of land have been bought up by other farmers and combined with their own land to make larger and more efficient farms, much of it has been gobbled up by newly affluent professional and managerial people living in the suburbs.

This land is often used as an investment or tax dodge and generally lies fallow rather than being worked. Since no one is living on it full time, such property often becomes a dumping ground—not so much for trash and kitchen garbage as for worn-out, hard-to-dispose-of heavyweights such as old tires, cars, appliances, heavy chunks of angle iron, metal screening, wire and all sorts of other bulky and heavy oddments made of iron or steel.

When it comes to survival, most animals are anything but dumb, especially an infinitely flexible, adaptable, edge-of-civilization-dwelling species like the cottontail. As this changing land-use pattern became more pronounced in secondary rings around major cities and also often around small towns, the local rabbitry quickly glommed onto the fact that these tortuous tangles of metal offered far better protection from predators—of both the two- and the four-legged persuasions—than the classic briar and berry-patch thickets. A rabbit can jam itself into these

When hunting junky areas such as this, don't give up too quickly. As long as your dog stays excited, give him a chance. Sometimes it takes twenty minutes or longer to finally flush out a sophisticated old cottontail determined to sit tight come what may.

cast-iron coverts so that no fox-, coon-, beagle or other hound can dig him out. With persistence and patience, however, the smaller terriers can often dig the rabbits out eventually. These little dogs can go many places that the rabbit can, and if they keep at it long enough, they can often psych out a rabbit that is actually safe in an impenetrable devil's pile.

There are some tricks to junk-pile hunting as there are to any other kind. Don't waste time on junk piles with burrows and tunnels beneath them. Fill up these back doors or avoid hunting those junk piles altogether. After a while you learn the different junk piles (each has its own character) and come to know the best producers. Many piles will never harbor more than one rabbit at a time. Others, due to their size and layout, are veritable apartment houses holding two, three or even four rabbits at once. It's also a good idea to "rest" a pile after harvesting it successfully. If it's a consistently good producer, another rabbit will usually take up residence within a few weeks to replace the one or two you shot out previously.

Though beagles aren't as effective at junk-pile hunting as the smaller, slimmer terriers, it's still a good idea to work promising-looking junk piles with the larger dogs occasionally. You never know what will happen. As long as the dog is interested in a pile, let him work on it, even if it takes twenty or thirty minutes. Chances are he smells a bunny in there. Often it helps if you walk around on top of the pile, jumping up and down a bit and maybe peeling off the top layer of debris to try to help flush the rabbit.

Junk-pile hunting isn't classic or elegant rabbit running, but the hunting is usually nearby, convenient and productive. Give it a try!

CLOTHING FOR RABBIT HUNTING

Rabbit hunting occurs at various times of the year in differing regions of the country under widely varying weather conditions. But one item is always a good idea for any rabbit hunter anywhere: a two-piece suit of long-legged and long-sleeved thermal underwear. The cotton waffle-weave type is inexpensive and available everywhere and serves admirably.

This inner layer of protection helps fend off the troublesome briars, nettles, prickers and stickers of all types that are an invariable part of good rabbit habitat. They also help keep you warm during the breezy and surprisingly chilly days of this fall and winter hunting sport. Slogging through wet streams and mud can often mean wet legs, and long johns help keep a wet hunter warmer and more comfortable than would otherwise be the case.

Nylon-faced "briar pants" are another good bet for bunny hunting, with or without a dog. Though hunting with a dog often means you don't have to negotiate as much thick and prickly cover as you would on your own, there always seem to be prickers about when hunting rabbits! These special hunting pants, available at any well-stocked sporting-goods store and at many of the larger sporting-goods sections in major department or discount stores, can protect tender shins and upper legs from a myriad of painful cuts and scratches.

For the upper body, I prefer a soft flannel shirt of cotton in moderate weather and wool or wool and synthetic blends in colder weather. If necessary, a light down jacket or heavier woolen "stag" shirt or cruiser jacket (20-ounce or heavier wool) will do well. The wool turns briars better and is warmer in dampish weather, but it's also heavier to carry around all day and it doesn't "breathe" as well if the hunter is perspiring heavily.

Lightweight six- or eight-inch-high leather "bird shooter" boots do well for most of this hunting. If it's wet going, you can use rubber boots, or if you're economy-minded, the lightweight slipover rubbers can convert leather boots to adequate footwear for less money. A scarf can protect your neck from chilling gusts of wind or, more important, from snow being dropped suddenly down the back of the neck when negotiating thick and tall cover laden with snowy stems.

A wide-brimmed western-type hat is nice during sunny, windy days afield, and the old-fashioned but very warm watch cap or stocking cap (or ski mask) works well on colder days. Sunglasses help if you are hunting in glaring snow or during very sunny days where there is a lot of glare. A ChapStick spares you the painful chapped lips that can seem to spring up in a matter of moments when working in cold, windy weather. Gloves or mittens usually aren't a good idea, since they slow down gun handling and make it less safe. Your hands can usually be kept warm in your pockets, one at a time, by rotating your gun from hand to hand when need be. If not, a pocket hand warmer serves nicely without interfering with your gun-handling effectiveness.

A small day pack or rucksack is often a good idea for all-day rabbit-hunting jaunts. In it you can comfortably carry your lunch, camera, extra film, and—if you're cunning—a clean dry pair of socks to use if needed.

Of course, no small game hunter of any type would be properly outfitted without an outer small game coat. This coat should be outsize so that it can fit loosely and comfortably even over bulky items like down or heavy woolen jackets. The fabric should be a close-woven, water-repellent, long-wearing, briar-turning canvas and should include larger outer pockets for ammunition and other goodies. It should also include a game bag, lined with a blood-proof rubber or other material with similar properties. This game bag can either be built into the coat itself, facing inward (a usually cheaper construction that holds more), or it can be a snap-on or zip-on facing-out bag that attaches to the back panel of the coat (handier and more convenient to get game in and out of and to doff when resting).

These coats come in countless designs, and since a good one (if taken care of) literally lasts a lifetime, you should take your time selecting what you want and, if necessary, pay a few dollars extra to get exactly what fits your needs. In hotter country, the rabbit hunter can get by well with a sleeveless vest, carrying a smaller game bag and with fewer pockets. These vests are cooler, lighter and cheaper, but they don't offer the protection, flexibility and capacity of the full coat.

GUNS AND AMMUNITION FOR RABBIT HUNTING WITH A DOG

While the non-dog-using rabbit hunter can sometimes get by easily with a .22 (by spotting napping rabbits on hillsides and shooting them at a fair distance on the sit), the dog-using hunter is better advised to stick with a shotgun, since the target is almost always shot while running full tilt for the next county.

Either a 12- or 20-gauge shotgun is fine (the 16-gauge being almost a dead item in this country as this is written). "High-based" or extra-powerful "magnum" loads aren't really necessary for this type of hunting. The prey usually isn't shot at inordinately long range, and rabbits aren't particularly bulletproof citizens. The trick is to *hit* the rabbit—once that's done it doesn't take as much to kill it as may be the case with squirrels and in some types of pheasant and waterfowl hunting. So standard-velocity loadings are fine and number 6 shot is—hands down—

52

the best size shot to use for rabbits under 98 percent of the field conditions in which they will be encountered. The larger number 5 shot isn't necessary for a clean kill, and it yields a more open pattern through which the rabbit may slip more easily. On the other hand, the number 7½ shot is getting a bit smallish to guarantee clean kills at a distance and in thick cover.

If the hunter is a youngster, the 20-gauge is probably the best choice of shotshell. Although most beginners starting young seem invariably to end up with a .410-caliber (not a true gauge) shotshell firing the heavy-duty 3-inch load, I don't recommend it. Though I myself killed my first rabbit with this "boy's gun," it kicks as much as a 20-gauge and, owing to the long, slim case, has far more shot deformation—meaning it just isn't as efficient in maintaining the pattern and thus killing.

If a youngster can't comfortably shoot a 2¾-inch low-based 20-gauge field load, more recoil-tolerant conditions obtaining when shooting at running game in a loose and relaxed fashion (as opposed to tight-shoulder target shooting), then he or she shouldn't be afield with *any* sort of scatter-gun. On the other hand, when the youngster can handle it and needs the extra power, a 20-gauge gun handling the longer 3-inch magnum-type loading will be a gun that, for all practical purposes, equals the power of the larger 12-gauge loading.

What type of gun is another subject. The single-shots are inexpensive and, in some respects, safer and lighter for a youngster to learn on. Though there is nothing wrong with using either a side-by-side or over-and-under double-barreled gun for either type of rabbit hunting, they generally don't get the nod since (other things being equal) they usually cost more than an equivalent pump- or slide-action gun or an autoloading ("automatic") smoothbore. The new Winchester models 1300 or 1500 are good rabbit guns. A particularly good beginner's choice is the Winchester Model 37A "Youth," which comes in either 20-gauge or .410 and offers a shorter, lighter-weight stock and barrel specially tailored for the smaller frames of youngsters. This inexpensive single-shot gun carries a rubber recoil pad for extra comfort, and the cost is reasonable indeed at significantly less than $100, depending upon where you buy it.

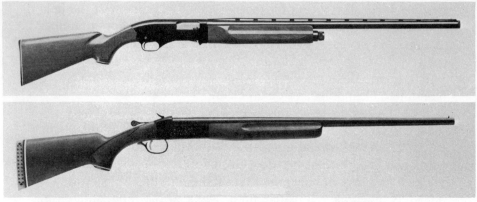

A good-quality medium-priced autoloading (or "automatic") shotgun like this Model 1500 Winchester (top), in either the 12 or 20 gauge, is a good all-around rabbit gun for any type of hunting with dogs.

To start small-framed youngsters out properly in the sport, shotguns specially scaled down in dimensions and weight, such as the Model 37A "Youth" by Winchester (below), are best. (Photos courtesy of WINCHESTER-WESTERN*)*

Rabbit hunting with a dog is a fast and exciting sport and one of the best ways to introduce a youngster to the outdoors. Best of all, it's an easy and inexpensive pastime that you can pursue almost anywhere in the country and at almost any time of the year, state laws allowing.

As you grow and mature in your appreciation of rabbit rousting with a beagle or other dog, you'll find yourself shooting fewer and fewer bunnies on the first few jumps and extending the hunt by letting the little yodel hounds push the rabbit around through the area. The dogs enjoy the sport so much and it's so much fun to watch them and listen to their music that it seems a shame to cut it all short with a premature kill. Billy Bibb always lets the rabbits who run the longest and best races *get away* and refuses even to shoot at them.

"Want them fellers to breed up more long-running rabbits just like them," he mused one day during a blustery January Alabama hunt. "After all, there's a world of difference between *hunting* and *killing*."

Amen.

3

The *Other* Rabbits

Thirty yards in front and to the right of me, a strange white-accented apparition exploded out from behind the brush and windmilled across the bare brown New Mexico plain. To my cottontail-trained eyes, this weirdo looked more like a small deer that was all legs rather than a rabbit—it was so huge and loped along in such a leggy, disjointed way. Nothing like the tight-packed scurry of the familiar mop-tail.

Since this was primarily a photo jaunt, the only gun I had with me on this western swing was a long-barreled single-action revolver in the hot little .22 WRF magnum caliber. I yelled to get my friend Mark's attention and powdered one off at our double-jointed friend before he made it safely to Colorado. Dust bloomed some six feet behind him and then he really cut into overdrive. I just *thought* he'd been running before. Another shot, though I swung a good six feet farther in front of him, was still about a yard behind the bobbing backside owing to the extra speed he'd poured on.

Then the deeper-throated *crack* of Mark's scope-sighted .243 rifle joined in, and a far larger eruption of tan-colored earth exploded at the very seat of the speeding black-tailed jackrabbit's pants. This caused him to angle more to the left and head almost straight out in front of us, thus making for a somewhat easier shot. Mark jacked another shell in, and while I held my fire (he was too far away from us for the short-legged pistol to be effective), he carefully sighted through the high-powered scope and touched it off again. The jack cartwheeled forward another ten feet and lay still.

Mark sauntered out to retrieve his prize, and as he ambled back toward me with the jack draped casually from his shoulder over his back, I was a bit astonished to note that the big hare's front feet dangled almost to Mark's knees, though its hind feet were nearly up at his shoulders. No cottontail rabbit this!

Actually, the "other" rabbits covered in this chapter aren't rabbits at all but hares. How do hares differ from rabbits? Well, they are larger, running from about twice on up to four or more times larger than the cottontail. Also, hares are born fully furred and with eyes open, whereas true rabbits aren't. Hares of all types have longer ears and longer legs and rely far more on running to elude their enemies. Rabbits, as we have seen, are primarily medium- to heavy-cover animals that, although they seem to be extremely fast runners, actually prefer to hide. When they do run, it is more of a darting, zigzag scamper or scurry designed to buy enough time to duck down a hole or into a thick brush pile or some other refuge where their pursuer can't follow. The hares, on the other hand, depend upon their speed to outdistance most enemies in a straightforward race, though they still can and do use their abilities to turn inside such speedsters as the coyote, which is the chief predator of the western jackrabbit.

There are several hares that are of no importance to the American sportsman. Largest of all is the arctic hare, which attains a length of 17 to 24 inches and a weight of 6 to 12 pounds and inhabits only a bleak belt of tundra in extreme northern Canada and the west coast of Greenland, far away from the hunting grounds of U.S. small game hunters. The Alaskan equivalent of this animal is the tundra hare, which is about the same length but a couple of pounds lighter, its range limited to the coast of northern and western Alaska. The European hare actually gets a bit longer than these two (at 25 to 27 inches) and weighs in at a right hefty 7 to 10 pounds. But hunting this introduced animal (the one that caused most of the old English and Scottish poaching stories, by the way) is limited to certain areas of New York State and not very avidly pursued even by hunters in this region.

The last of the lesser hares is another outsized type, the

Jackrabbits are actually hares, not true rabbits at all, and to hunters used to cottontails they look gigantic. Extra-long legs and ears make them appear even larger than they are.

antelope jack of extreme southwestern New Mexico and a smallish area of southern Arizona. This fellow reaches a length of 19 to 21 inches and a hefty weight of 6 to 13 pounds. Too restricted in range to be considered a staple variety for the American small game hunter (it's more a Mexican species), the antelope jack does have the distinction of sporting the longest ears of all the North American hares—truly huge even by jackrabbit standards.

The three animals we are interested in are the black-tailed and white-tailed jackrabbits and the "snowshoe rabbit" or vary-

57

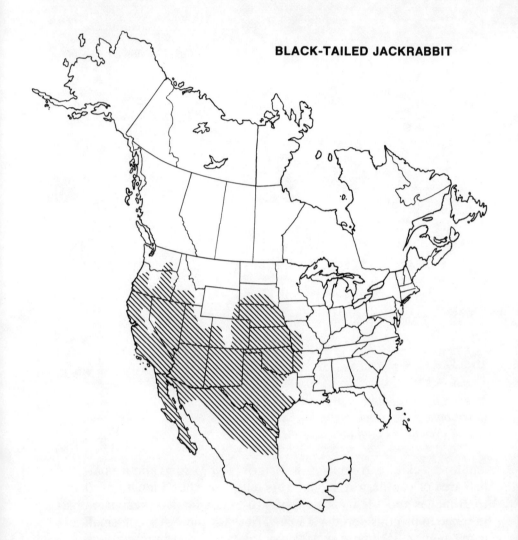

BLACK-TAILED JACKRABBIT

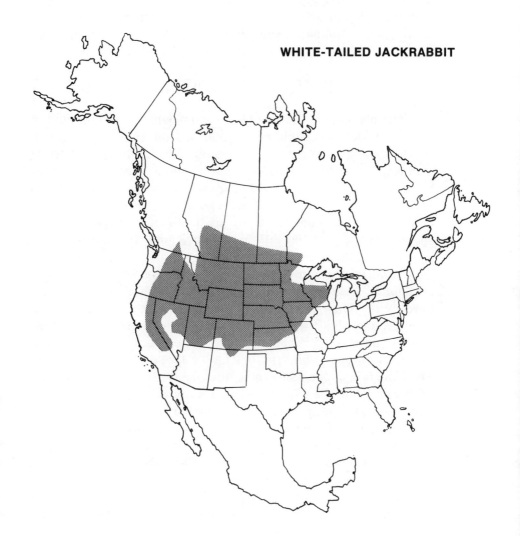

WHITE-TAILED JACKRABBIT

ing hare. The first two are much alike, and the sport involved in hunting them is quite similar. They are western open- and dry-country rifleman's targets, while the snowshoe is a northern snow-country animal, involving a quite different kind of hunting.

HUNTING THE JACKRABBITS

The blacktail is the smaller and somewhat more common of the two widely available jacks (named from their similarity to the long-eared jackass, by the way). Blacktails run 17 to 21 inches in length and weigh from 3 to 7 pounds, not much heavier but a good bit longer than the true swamp rabbit. Whitetails run only about an inch longer but are a good bit chunkier, at a weight of from 5 to 10 pounds. Both are fast-running open-country speedsters that test the skill of any dedicated rifleman.

The whitetail ranges the northern plains and the western high country of the mountain areas, while the blacktail is more an animal of the open-country grasslands of the central and lower West. How to tell them apart when they overlap? Aside from the fact that the whitetail is larger and more heavily built, its ears run about 5 inches in length rather than 6 inches and are not black-tipped, while the blacktail's ears do sport black tips. The blacktail, as the name indicates, always has black on the top of its tail, while the whitetail almost never does. And, finally, the whitetail has eight mammae while the blacktail has only six.

The blacktail remains grayish-brown in color all year, while the whitetail does turn white or pale gray in the winter, especially in the upper part of its range. But there is no problem telling the winter-coated whitetail from the snowshoe, because of the extra-long ears and legs and larger size of the former. Also, the whitetail maintains a dark buff color at the base of its hair, although the hair must be separated to see this.

Jackrabbits, like cottontails, do not dig burrows but occupy forms scattered throughout their territories. Jacks are also homebodies and will not leave their home range unless forced to by severe drought. But whereas the cottontail's home ground is a few acres, that of the larger and wider-ranging jack is about four square miles.

60

Over most of its range a jackrabbit such as this one will change color in the winter, as does the varying or "snowshoe" hare. Blending with the winter's snow helps them evade one of their primary enemies, the golden eagle. (Photo courtesy of WYOMING FISH & GAME DEPARTMENT*)*

Jacks will eat just about anything green that grows, from the various grasses, weedy plants and shrubs on through sagebrush, prickly pear cactus, mesquite and greasewood. Where jacks compete directly with sheep and cattle they can be a serious problem, and biologists have estimated that a dozen jacks eat as much as an adult sheep and sixty jacks as much as a steer. Helping to control their numbers, which at times reach pestilential proportions, is a positive service the hunter performs.

Coyotes are the jackrabbit's chief predator, and those areas where the little brush wolves were poisoned out have sometimes shown jackrabbit population explosions highly detrimental to livestock interests. While a cottontail's top speed is only about 22 to 25 miles per hour, the jacks can easily hit 30 to 35 mph and if they really push it can reach the firewall speeds of 40 to 45 mph. That's faster than a full-grown elk or mule deer can run, and it provides a challenging target for even the most expert of riflemen.

Since jacks inhabit open country, they often feed at night, especially during the full moon. The hunter is advised to hunt early and late in the day, and better yet on days after darkish nights. Actually, jackrabbit hunting is more of a *shooting* sport than a *hunting* sport in that the usual drill is for the hunter to locate good country and then walk the animals up, shooting at them on the run. The blacktail is the warier of the two, usually getting up much farther out, while the whitetail sometimes explodes almost from under the hunter's feet like a cottontail.

Good jackrabbit country is easy enough to locate simply by asking the local farmers and ranchers. And they are almost all to eager to have you hunt them and help control them on their land!

Jacks are relatively big, thick-skinned animals with a lot of vitality. Also, owing to the nature of the open country they inhabit, it is often possible to get two or three running shots at the same animal, with the last shot being quite long. The .22-caliber rimfire rifles are simply too under-strength for this kind of hunting. They don't pack the punch for clean kills since the animals may be hit almost anywhere and at any range. Even the hopped-up .22 WRF magnum and the 5mm Remington magnum aren't ideal for this hunting.

This kind of sport really comes into its own with the hotter .22-caliber centerfire rifles and the intermediate class of .243, 6mm and .257 Roberts class of cartridge. Actually, the big game hunter can readily adapt any rifle from the .270 30/06 class even on up to the powerhouses like the 7mm and .30-caliber magnums for this kind of use. It provides ideal practice for the big game hunter and it's a heck of a lot of fun. Anyone who can hit a fair percentage of hotfooting jacks with a scope-sighted centerfire rifle won't have much trouble hitting a bounding deer at the same range!

Jacks are not the best of eating, generally being stringy and a bit strong in flavor. Younger animals, however, if soaked in salt water and parboiled, can be made reasonably palatable, though you'll know that no cottontail is on the table.

62

Jackrabbit hunting is not only a rifleman's sport but is basically for the centerfire rifle, because of the extra power often needed for longer-range shots against these surprisingly tough animals. A good choice is the Winchester Model 70 in .22 or .24 caliber, with a good vari-power scope such as a 2x–7x model. (Photo courtesy of WINCHESTER-WESTERN)

THE VARYING HARE OR "SNOWSHOE RABBIT"

This animal is a true hare also and, though smaller than the jacks, is about twice the size of a cottontail. Its range is usually about a square mile and the animal is a speedy runner, relying on those outsized ("snowshoe") rear feet to keep it bounding along on the crust of the snow without breaking through to where the going would be much rougher and where it would be far more vulnerable to both heat loss and predators. Snowshoes are subject to great peaks and valleys in their population densities, though no one has yet been able to explain just what triggers these remarkable cycles. When the animal does "crash," related predators, especially the lynx, crash right along with it.

Though snowshoes aren't nearly as fast as the dry-country jacks, they can make 30 miles per hour or a bit more when pressed, which is considerably faster than the various cottontails—and this is over snow, so it is usually adequate to avoid four-legged enemies, even though the latter may have a faster initial burst of speed. Snowshoes can safely bound over crusted snow that will not hold the heavier bobcat or the larger-footed but still heavier lynx.

In the Far North or high up in the mountains, the snowshoe is truly "the bread of the woods" in that about everything feeds upon it, including all sorts of winged predators (great horned owl, snowy owl, goshawk, gyrfalcon, Cooper's hawk, barred owl and great gray owl) as well as mammalian predators (lynx, fox, weasel, wolverine, mink, fisher, bobcat and coyote).

Hunting these medium-sized hares is usually done one of two ways. The hunter can track them through snow (using snow-shoes or cross-country skis if the snow is deep enough) or look for the napping animal in its form out on the sunny southern exposures of the ravines and hillsides. This sport is a solitary one for the rifleman. It calls for quiet stalking, strong legs and a good pair of binoculars. You should wear a white suit and even wrap your gun in white if possible. This is challenging sport, but it is not as productive as hunting with a dog (except in extremely densely populated regions).

Dog hunting is also quite popular, especially in the United States. Though some devotees might disagree with me, hunting snowshoes with dogs is quite similar to running cottontails with beagles, except that in deep snow areas a larger dog can often hunt better and harder. This is usually a shotgunner's sport, since the quarry is most always hit running full tilt and fairly close in.

Snowshoes are reasonably good to eat, but their meat carries little or no fat and so is a bit dry and stringy. It's best to serve them liberally seasoned in a stew rather than to fry or roast them up on their own.

4

Scoring on Gray and Fox Squirrels

A persistent scratching-scrabbling noise in the drying leaves behind me brought me out of a deep sleep. I almost yawned and stretched before I caught myself. It was a temptation to close my heavily lidded eyes and drift back off. I had been out in the open woods most of the day, and between the walking and the waiting in the blustery fall wind, I was plenty tired.

I was so comfortable, leaning back against the towering oak trunk behind and well padded all around with a veritable foam-rubber contour couch where I had wormed my way deep into a pile of still fragrant dry leaves. Then it came again, closer this time. Surely *that* couldn't be one of the elusive will-o'-the-wisp gray squirrels I had been vainly searching for all day. Too loud for sure!

Then again it came, still closer. I strained my eyes around to the right. About the time I thought they might come unzipped and fall out on the ground in front of me, I caught a flicker of motion about fifteen feet to my extreme right. A second later, a scampering, coiled spring of an animal moved fully into view. He stopped, twitched and cocked his head this way and that, sensing that something wasn't quite right.

I desperately tried not to breathe but failed. I did succeed in not blinking, however. The little animal cocked a beady eye my way and bobbed its head up and down. Many years later I was to learn that this head bobbing is a typical squirrel mannerism to aid in judging distance. That ability is so vitally important to these fast-running, long-jumping little tree dwellers that, in addition to using their superb basic vision, they have also learned to make use of parallax (the apparent change in position of an object when viewed from different angles or directions) in order to judge distances and objects even more accurately. Though I hadn't moved, this guy knew that there was something fishy about me and was calling on every trick he knew to figure out what it was!

The squirrel circled warily and began edging farther away from me as I frantically tried to figure out what to do. I had never shot a squirrel and was every bit as cotton-mouthed about the whole affair as I was when, almost a quarter of a century to the day later, I shot and killed my first grizzly bear. Dimly I realized that I must do *something,* since the alarmed squirrel was ready to bolt at any instant.

Like one of those weirdly floundering monsters in a grade-B Japanese horror movie, I lurched wildly to my feet on benumbed legs made of unfeeling straw. As I thrashed and struggled to come fully erect, bring the gun well up and line it in on the squirrel, my elusive little target took off through the leaves for another big oak tree nearby. Just as I thought I could squeeze off a shot with the 12-gauge shotgun that was far and away too big for my bony nine-year-old frame, the bottom dropped out and I fell right down almost on my nose. I had simply asked too much of those cold, numb legs as I tried to stand up, swivel half around and let off a shot all in one motion.

The agony of defeat. I lay there with disappointment a hot bile in my throat. All day hunting and the only fair chance I'd had, and this was the way it ended up. I hadn't even had the fun of shooting and missing. Just falling down ignominiously like a bulldogged steer. The shame of it! And yet, as I reflect back on that galling episode many years later, it seems to be peculiarly indicative of what was to come over the years of squirrel hunting that followed. For this strange, ultra-three-dimensional type of hunting (where up and down are at least as important as right and left) is always full of its special brand of surprises, disappointments and triumphs. (In the years to come they didn't *all* get away.)

Squirrel hunting occupies a strong second place, nation-wide, among small game hunters. In some areas of the Southeast and the Midwest the squirrel even outdistances the front-running cottontail rabbit in popularity among sportsmen. And why not? The quarry is challenging, resourceful and widely available. And squirrel stew and squirrel potpie are two of the most toothsome treats ever served up on a cold winter day.

But what do we mean when we talk about squirrel hunting? We don't mean pursuit of the various little nocturnal tree squirrels that are too small to be classified as game animals. Nor do we mean that scolding little chatterbox, the highly aggressive little red squirrel, which is not considered to be a game animal by most, though it is a daytime (diurnal) animal. And in this instance we are not considering the various ground squirrels (covered briefly in chapter 6), which constitute an entirely different type of secondary sport. No, for our purposes we mean the gray squirrel and the eastern fox squirrel—both true tree squirrels and both fascinating little game animals. To hunt them successfully and enjoyably we must learn about them and how they live.

THE GRAY SQUIRRELS

Though there are other tree squirrels in our country, the three gray squirrels and the eastern fox squirrel are the important game animals of this clan. Of the three gray squirrels, the eastern is the smallest, the most widespread and far and away the most important game animal. These energetic little animals are 8 to 10 inches in body length and sport a large, bushy tail (necessary for balancing properly during their high-altitude gymnastics in the trees) that adds another 7¾ to 10 inches in length. They weigh from 12 to 25 ounces when mature, with animals in the northern part of their range running larger than those in the Deep South. Though the three gray squirrels are technically considered three different species, in practical sporting terms they are close enough in appearance and habit to be considered the same animal for our purposes. However, since squirrel hunting east of the Mississippi has always been far more important and popular than it has been farther west, most of our comments about squirrel hunting will be focused on this eastern

GRAY SQUIRRELS

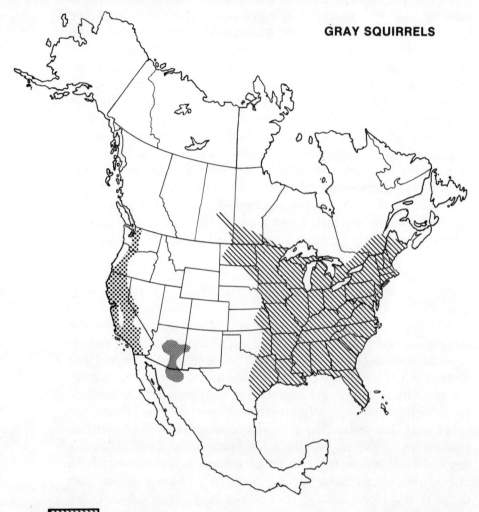

 Eastern Gray Squirrel

 Western Gray Squirrel

 Arizona Gray Squirrel

animal. Though Westerners have tended to overlook the sporting possibilities of the gray squirrel, more and more of them (especially in California) are coming to recognize what they have been missing.

The Arizona gray squirrel runs slightly larger than its eastern cousin, averaging up to 3 or 4 inches longer and weighing 2 to 6 ounces more. This is the most restricted in range of the three grays, and the least hunted. Pursuing these animals with dogs is almost totally unknown, though it is fairly prevalent farther east.

The western gray squirrel occupies a rather narrow east-west range that curves like a crescent up and down the entire west coast of the southern forty-eight states. This is the largest of the three grays, weighing up to 2 to 3 ounces more than comparable Arizona animals and running an inch or two longer. This animal divides its time more equally between the trees and the ground, while the Arizona gray is the most arboreal (tree dwelling) of the three and the eastern gray spends more time on the ground than the other two.

Though there is no such thing as a "dull" or uninteresting animal, the gray squirrel is particularly fascinating. Unlike most mammals, it is strongly diurnal and usually moves abroad only between dawn and dusk. Its large, dark eyes are well adapted to the peculiar demands of its arboreal life-style in that the retina is completely comprised of cone cells (unlike our retina, which is a mixture of cone and rod cells, and unlike the eyes of most nocturnal birds and mammals, which are largely comprised of rod cells). These cone cells provide outstanding ability to distinguish fine detail and also mean that the gray squirrel has far faster reactions than we or most other mammals can muster. Animals that move fast need this faster accommodation—especially in the squirrel's case, since it needs to sense potential attacks from *below* as well as from above or beside its position.

Interestingly enough, though the squirrel's eyes have only the daylight-oriented cone cells, their adaptation to the dark is about the same as ours. Occasionally, gray squirrels will be found feeding in a brightly moonlit cornfield, and it has been found that they are most active when the incident light ranges from 150 to 650 foot candles—the brightness of early morning

The gray squirrel is especially wary when on the ground because then the animal is at a disadvantage—and knows it. (Photo courtesy of WYOMING FISH & GAME DEPARTMENT)

and late afternoon on clear days and all day long on cloudy, overcast days. This is a note for the squirrel hunter's journal—the best time to hunt grays is the first two hours of daylight and the last two hours of afternoon light on clear days. If you want to make an all-day outing of your trip and you hanker for results, be sure to pick a cloudy, soggy day with low light levels.

The squirrel has a very large field of vision, which is vital to an animal that is frequently preyed upon by others. The eyes are set into the head so that they allow more than 40 degrees of forward-binocular (three-dimensional) vision to better judge distances and solidity of objects (to land upon when running and jumping at top speed). Though most animals have a blind spot at or near the center of their eyes, the squirrel's eyes are arranged so that its blind spot occurs in the lower third of its vision, allowing it to have an uninterrupted image of the sky, where most attacks come from. Not only do squirrels see extremely well, they have exceptionally keen noses, and it has been proven that they locate buried nuts by scent rather than by memory of where they buried their own. Thus, burying food is of benefit to the species in general (as well as a positive conservation benefit because of resultant reforestation) rather than to any one digger. In other words, squirrels don't tend to reclaim their own specially buried food but feed on any that they can locate.

The gray squirrel lives in a three-dimensional world, and any attempt to map this world without taking into consideration both vertical paths and horizontal ones results in an incomplete picture at best. Grays generally prefer fairly open woods, usually near a winding stream or some sort of water, whose branches provide airborne travel lanes from one end of the wood to the other. Hardwood areas are preferred, though in the South they do live in piney woods. Open oak and hickory forests with a light understory of hazel, hawthorn and dogwood provide squirrels with the ideal food (so they can spend much time foraging among the forest floor litter for nuts, mushrooms and fruits) and yet with enough cover for protection. A wooded area with a fair ratio of older trees providing an abundance of cavities for safe nesting is preferred above all others. Natural holes, if they meet the squirrel's exacting standards for a home, are preferred to leaf nests, since the former afford more protection from most enemies and somewhat better shelter.

It's not always an easy thing to see the entrance to a den. Sometimes these are quite small—only 3 to 4 inches in diameter—but you can usually see where the squirrels have gnawed the bark around the rim of the hole. Often a protruding scar on the trunk with a narrow darker streak on the bark below is a giveaway to a den entrance. The very large, ragged holes in a tree usually mean entrances to panic stations and temporary hides, not true dens. Large holes in the base of a tree, often leading to a considerable hollow reaching far up into the tree trunk, are escape holes, not den entrances. Incidentally, the squirrel's whiskers, which protrude about 3 inches from the face, serve to inform the fatter fellows when they might have too tight a squeeze clambering into a small hole or hollow.

When there is a lack of appropriate natural hollows, squirrels resort to building leaf nests. These are usually ragged balls of sticks, leaves and twigs from 1 to 2 feet in diameter, and they can be surprisingly strong and sturdy in their own right. At least one nest has been known to last upwards of six years, but these nests do require constant repair and maintenance, and once abandoned they fall quickly to pieces. Any nest that looks in good repair is probably still in use. Sighting a number of these nests in a woodlot is a dead giveaway that it is a good squirrel wood. The nests are usually wedged securely in the fork of a tree or out along a major branch. *You should never fire into a nest just to see what happens*. This is not sporting, and you can cause the injury or death of one or more squirrels, including young ones, which are never recovered.

Though gray squirrels, especially the eastern types, spend much of their time on the ground foraging for food, they are twice as alert when out of their trees. They are relatively slow, easy-to-hit targets scampering on the ground, and they cannot afford to spend much time hunched over food in places where vegetation obscures the view. Thus squirrels prefer to eat at table—usually old stumps or low but large limbs from which they can get a more elevated and less obstructed view of their surroundings. They'll often eat with their backs against the main tree trunk to protect themselves from danger in the rear.

When scouting for a good squirrel-hunting area, survey all large stumps carefully for the fresh litter from squirrel meals such as nutshells, acorn bits or scales from pine cones. Look for squirrel travel lanes, which in a well-populated squirrel wood are rather clearly marked with claw marks on the tree bark, fallen logs or rail fences. Check rough-bark trees more carefully than smooth-skinned trees like beech or birch, since squirrel claws find much better purchase on the rough-surfaced wood. When they do climb the smoother-barked trees, however, the claw marks will be much more prominent: longer slip scratches run-

72

ning up to 3 and 4 inches in length where the claws have slipped until they obtained solid purchase.

Though gray squirrels are normally satisfied to spend their entire lives in an area of ten acres or less, under extreme stress of occasional population explosions they have been known to migrate for long distances. They are extremely energetic animals and on a normal day are up by dawn, feeding or gathering and storing food for future use. They are such hardy and adaptable animals that it is difficult to hurt a strong colony by hunting. Tree-climbing snakes are their greatest enemies, with hawks and owls ranking next (though red and gray foxes, bobcats, raccoons and house cats and dogs all take an occasional squirrel).

The gray squirrel is relatively long-lived for such a small animal. Captive squirrels sometimes reach the ripe old age of fifteen to twenty years (similar to a grizzly bear or a caribou under captive conditions). Maximum age in the wild, however, is more realistically set at around six to eight years. Though eastern gray squirrels today do not begin to equal the numbers that existed prior to 1700, when the entire eastern part of the United States was covered with an almost uninterrupted dense mature hardwood forest (with the preferred oak probably the most common species of tree), there are still many millions of squirrels that are, for the most part, considerably underharvested by sportsmen.

THE EASTERN FOX SQUIRREL

The fox or "cat" squirrel is the largest of our tree squirrels, and while it has many overall similarities to the smaller gray squirrels, it also offers a considerable contrast in some respects. The eastern fox is a substantially larger animal than the gray, reaching a length of 28 inches and, at an adult weight of from 1½ to 3 pounds, running from twice to three times the size. Fox squirrels reach their largest size in the more northerly parts of their range. Unlike the gray, where the sexes are identical in size, the female fox squirrel is in many cases a bit larger than the male.

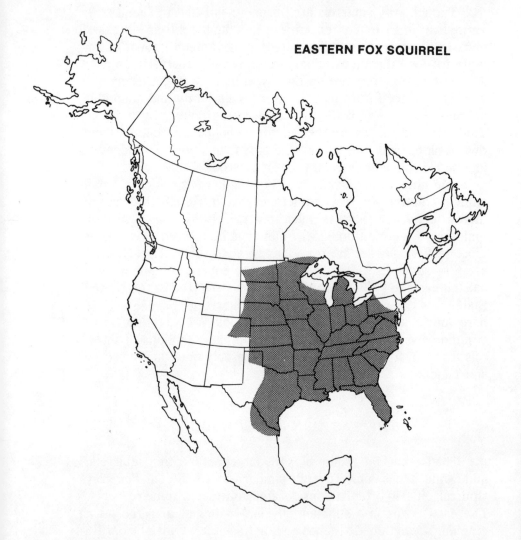

EASTERN FOX SQUIRREL

Though distinguishing a small fox squirrel from a large gray can at times cause a bit of confusion for the beginner, there are some easily checked distinctions. In profile, the plane of the fox squirrel's head from nose to ear is straighter than that of the gray, giving the fox a more flat-headed look. The fox is usually reddish or reddish brown in color, and the bones of a fox squirrel (if you are dressing one out) are pinkish, while those of the gray are white. Perhaps it's easier to remember that the fox squirrel has the reddish hair and the reddish bones. The gray squirrel has two more teeth, with a total of twenty-two compared to the fox squirrel's total of twenty. Usually size and coloration are enough to tell the animals apart.

There are also considerable behavioral differences between these two important types of squirrels. The fox is a much more daylight-oriented animal, preferring ten times as much light as the gray. In practical sporting terms, this means that fox squirrels are not usually out and around as early or late in the day and it is much better to hunt them on clearer, brighter days rather than the overcast low-light days preferred by the gray. Fox squirrels are hardly ever out foraging for food after dark even on the brightest moonlit nights, so full-moon nights have no meaning for the fox-squirrel hunter, whereas for the gray-squirrel seeker (especially if the days have been unseasonably hot or wet) a full-moon period may imply bad hunting the following day because the squirrels have been out feeding at night.

The fox squirrel, as one might suspect from its larger size, is not the agile aerialist in the trees that the gray or smaller non-game red squirrels are. When pursued, the fox squirrel is much more likely than the gray to run longer distances on the ground before taking to the trees. Of the three, the red squirrel (weighing only a scant 5 to 11 ounces and thus not providing enough size to be an edible game animal in most people's judgment) is by far the most aggressive. Though these small squirrels prefer coniferous forests in the Appalachians, they are at home in the hardwood forests. Where they overlap the grays, the reds will often bluff the latter away from prime feeding grounds.

The fox squirrel is not as shy and wary as the gray. Though tamed fox squirrels often get to the point where they may be

The fox squirrel is larger and less of a tree dweller than the gray squirrel . . . but is equally good on the table! (Photo by Leonard Lee Rue III)

handled and stroked, this is very rare with grays, and although gray squirrels can become rather confiding in certain backyard or park situations, they never lose as much of their instinctive wildness as fox squirrels do.

Though both squirrels like to lie out in the sun, the later-rising fox squirrel is much more prone to do this and to be out stirring around during the brightest of midday periods. While the gray squirrel is a creature of denser, more mature forests, the

76

fox squirrel prefers more open woodlands and gets by very well in smaller stands of trees. The fox squirrel must have trees to den in and to flee to for safety, but these can easily be very small groups of trees or even isolated ones. The latter, being more out in the open, receive more sunlight and thus produce larger nut crops to satisfy the animal's requirements for food and preferences for high-light situations. The fox squirrel needs only a couple of such trees to be content. It extracts a far higher percentage of its water requirements directly from the food it eats, and thus it is not as closely tied as the gray to the "bottoms" and winding stream courses. In fact, in areas where the fox squirrel does inhabit larger forests, it prefers to stay up on the drier, brighter and more open ridge tops and leave the denser, wetter bottoms to the gray squirrel.

Fox squirrels are active at all times of the year and during almost any kind of weather. Their larger size makes them more heat-efficient than the gray, and they can stand the cold better. They seldom den up during bitter weather as the grays often do. Fox squirrels, like grays, have a strong penchant for field corn, and open woodland edges along prime cornfields are often good spots to search for fox-squirrel grounds. Incidentally, neither squirrel eats the entire corn kernel; they just take the germ end and let the starchy portion go to waste. One way to determine if the corn litter around a woods edge is made by a raccoon or other prowler rather than a squirrel is to check this factor. A litter of golden bits of corn is a dead giveaway that the corn-napping has been done by squirrels and is fresh and recent.

In the northeastern part of the fox squirrel's range, the animal tends toward a more grayish coloration and sometimes looks almost like an oversized gray, with rusty markings along its flanks and, of course, that less rounded facial profile. Toward the south they generally tend to get darker and blacker looking. (There is more color variation among the *typical* fox squirrel than among the gray, if one disregards the occasional atypical black or white gray squirrel encountered.) But the tip of the fox squirrel's long plumed tail is usually orange or reddish, while the gray's is white.

While fox squirrels undoubtedly were never as numerous as

grays, they are no longer found in the Northeast as extensively as they once were, although they do appear to be expanding their range in the Midwest a bit. Still a common and widely available game animal, it does not seem to be prospering as well as the gray squirrel in the modern era. With its habitat preference tending toward the more open, smaller woodlots, it would seem to be a "civilization prone" animal, well adapted to man and his ax and plow. And, in fact, it does appear to have prospered in a number of localized areas. Overall, however, the gray squirrel appears to have adapted to man a bit better. Perhaps this is owing to the gray's somewhat more alert and energetic ways. The less wary fox squirrel appears to be more vulnerable to hunting pressure and some other types of predation.

METHODS OF HUNTING SQUIRRELS WITHOUT DOGS

The two basic methods of hunting bushy-tails without canine help are "still-hunting" and "stand hunting." The classic beginner's squirrel hunt is for the youngster to go out alone with a .22 rifle, moving slowly through the woods, trying to surprise a feeding or foraging squirrel on the ground or on a low limb. This hunting is easy to participate in, since almost any patch of small, scrubby woodland bordering farm fields will do, whether it harbors squirrels or not—and many times it doesn't. The gun is usually a .22, since they are inexpensive, easily available and not costly to shoot.

There's nothing particularly wrong with this approach except that a .22 is somewhat mismatched to the hunting, because no matter how stealthy the moving hunter, the shots are usually at an alarmed, running target.

Still-Hunting

In still-hunting for squirrels, the hunter moves quietly and *slowly* through the woods. The primary mistake made in this type of hunting is to equate movement with hunting and go much too fast. You should work slowly, ever so s-l-o-w-l-y, through the woods. Pick an early morning or late afternoon period, with usually the first hour or hour and a half of daylight the preferred time. The best day for this is damp and overcast, when the leaves and other debris on the forest floor will be spongy and quiet to walk on. It is simply impossible for a hunter, however accomplished he or she may be, to sneak up on sharp-eyed and sharp-eared squirrels on a brittle, tinder-dry day. If the woods are "loudmouthed," still-hunting isn't the best way to get the makings for a squirrel mulligan.

The hunter should advance only two to four steps at a time. Take each step slowly and cautiously, being sure of exact foot placement on the forest floor. Don't ever step without knowing exactly what your foot will tread on, and transfer your weight from one foot to the other slowly and gingerly, so that if a sabotaging stick or leaf starts to snap or crunch, you can backpedal and place your front foot in another, safer place. Every four or five steps, pause entirely and remain quite still. Remember, you are looking for a smallish, rather neutral-colored quarry that can be anywhere *above* as well as around you. You must continually scan the woods in all directions, looking for that telltale flicker of a snappily waving plumed tail or a fast-decamping animal that has already spotted you.

At all times, be prepared to fire your gun quickly and safely. Carry it in both hands with one finger near (but not on) the trigger and the other positively reinforcing the safety mechanism by holding it on OFF or SAFE. You may only have an instant to fire, so be ready! As you move, listen carefully. Squirrels are noisy little fellows, especially if not alarmed. It is often possible for the alert hunter to hear them sharply chattering and scolding each other as they dispute territory at the other end of a small woods before the hunter has ever seen them.

When you are still-hunting, it's a safe bet that for every squirrel you see, three more will see you and get away without your ever knowing they were there. Furthermore, of the four squirrels you do see, probably three will have already seen you, and thus you'll be taking some sort of running shot. A scattergun is far and away better than a .22 rifle for this type of hunting, especially if the squirrel is up in a tree, because the shotgun with its more limited range makes for much safer shooting. Number 6

Look for small creeks surrounded by open hardwood areas when trying to locate good gray-squirrel hunting areas. This young hunter will follow the stream, looking for nests, nut fragments and the scampering squirrels themselves.

or even number 5 shot is the ticket for squirrels. They are tough-skinned, tenacious little animals with a lot of vitality. To knock one down out of a tree (sometimes from a great height) and to kill it cleanly takes a lot of power. If the hunter can absorb the extra recoil and muzzle blast, high-base or high-velocity shells are recommended. If a smallish youngster or a particularly gun-shy adult is involved, the recommendation is to go to number 5 shot and be limited to close to medium shots no farther than 20 or 25 yards out. Never go smaller than number 6 shot when hunting squirrels.

Fast shooting is often the case when still-hunting, so a pump or autoloader is preferred over a single-shot or a double-barreled gun. The choke should be modified or full, depending upon the hunting conditions. Modified is recommended for closer shots in thicker woods where its larger pattern ensures more hits. Full-choked guns, on the other hand, reach out farther for longer shots and serve to increase the hunter's effective range—other things being equal—about 5 to 7 yards. One of the adjustable choking devices serves well here to make the gun more flexible.

Squirrels like to be abroad on cool to medium days, and when the temperature is below 30 degrees Fahrenheit and above 65, or when the wind has a velocity of more than 6 miles per hour continuously, still-hunters can better occupy themselves in other activities. The squirrels won't likely be out and around in enough numbers to furnish good sport.

When moving through the woods in still-hunting, you are well advised to wear quiet clothing of wool or wool blends and stay away from the raspy, scratchy nylon and Dacron blends. Even cotton jeans can be too loud on a quiet day. Squirrels are exceptionally keen eyed, also, and seem to have a bit more color perception than most animals. Only man and the great apes have full color vision. However, while squirrels don't have true trichromatic color capabilities (their red-seeing mechanism in particular seems markedly different from ours) it has been demonstrated that they do have some limited color-resolving visual ability. Thus you should wear neutral-toned clothing (if blaze orange or other highly visible clothing is not required by your state's laws) and seek out camouflage patterns.

Stand Hunting

In this quieter, more contemplative type of hunting, you seek out a good spot and sit "on stand" as immobile as the trees around you, waiting for your quarry to come to you. The best way to do this is to be in the woods before dawn, using a small flashlight to find your way, so that you can be on stand at dawn's first light, when the squirrels begin stirring around. Of course, if your quarry is fox squirrels, then it isn't necessary to be abroad quite so early.

In either event, you should know where you are going. You should have pre-scouted your stands well before the hunting begins so that you can go straight to them and begin hunting. Looking for stand spots isn't the thing to do during the actual hunt. Thus, whether you are going to still-hunt or stand hunt or both, you should spend some pre-hunting-season days securing permission to hunt and locating good "squirrelly" woods. For gray squirrels, you should check along watercourses and pay particular attention to what trees are available. A small handbook on trees illustrating the different types of leaves is usually readily available at the nearest bookstore.

Though squirrels feed off a large variety of trees, they do have preferences. White oak and beech are two of their favorites and will be chosen first. Black oaks apparently yield acorns somewhat more bitter than white oaks, but if the latter aren't available then the black oaks will be utilized. Red-oak acorns are more bitter than those of black oaks and even lower in preference.

Bitterness is caused by tannin, and it appears that even individual trees will vary in how tasty their acorns are. Thus, when scouting woods for squirrels, always note those white oaks that show considerable feeding activity—acorn shells around them that have been gnawed by squirrels and scratch marks on the tree trunks. These favored trees will literally be squirrel incubators and, even though squirrels are shot out of them, more will move in if the tree is "rested" a bit between hunts.

Though squirrels are excellent swimmers and don't mind plunging into the water to get from here to there, they don't like to get wet unless necessary. Thus, they aren't usually out in the rain, even in a fine misting precipitation, and they usually aren't afield if the snow is more than two inches deep. Snow and ice hamper movement both on the ground and up in the trees and tend to exhaust the squirrels faster, making them burn up more energy than they would probably ingest from the food they sought out. Though squirrels have been known to dig through as much as a foot of snow to gather some buried nuts, this is hard and wearing work—especially if there is a crust of ice that must be broken through. So in many ways a dampish and overcast but not wet day is best for either still or stand hunting.

Warm clothing is vital when stand hunting. Since the hunter is not moving, the *apparent* cold is twice as great as it is for the

82

slowly moving still-hunter—especially if there is any sort of gusting wind or if the hunter's bottom becomes cold and damp from sitting on the damp ground. Down coats and multiple layers of clothing (much warmer than one or two exceptionally heavy garments) ranging from long underwear through warm shirts and sweaters are a good idea. Pocket hand warmers help during especially cold periods. A shivering hunter is a dead giveaway to the gimlet-eyed little tree runners. Quiet clothing is not so important here, since the hunter is supposedly only moving when shifting to another stand.

The stand hunter should remain absolutely still and silent. That means no smoking, no scratching, no throat clearing, no shivering, no body shifting of any type. The only limited movement that should ever be allowed is an occasional ultra-slow head turn to scan another quadrant of the forest that was hidden previously from view. If I am in a squirrelly woods, I try to make it for at least twenty minutes without a movement of any sort whatsoever. After that I will allow myself to turn my head about every ten or fifteen minutes to scan a new area. If the stand is a proven producer, I'll usually give it an hour, but after that I'll move on. After shooting once from a stand, it's usually time to move on and set up shop in another spot.

Though there is no hard and fast rule about how far apart stands must be, remember that squirrels can be surprisingly dense in good squirrel country with plenty of den trees and water and a nice cornfield nearby to supplement the wild foods. In these cases squirrels can occupy a range of as little as an acre or a bit less. Thus, some stands that are within 400 yards (about a quarter of a mile) of each other can be productively hunted back to back. It certainly isn't always necessary to pick up and completely change locales by automobile once you have shot a time or two at the end of a fairly large patch of woods. The smart hunter usually tries the other end of the same woods, circling around the field's edge and reentering the woods farther down rather than walking right through the woods themselves.

The stand hunter should, like the still-hunter, keep gun in hand in firing position at all times. Don't put your hands in your pockets to keep them warm and then have to fumble with the gun and lose that crucial split second that sometimes makes the difference between squirrel in the pot and an empty game bag. If your hands tend to get cold, use an old trick of mine and cut the fingers out of a pair of gloves from the fingertips back to the knuckle joints. They will be almost as warm as before and yet enable you to handle a gun very well. Keeping a hand warmer in your lap also helps, as long as the hand warmer isn't *too* warm.

The stand hunter must be more patient than the still-hunter. This implies a bit more mature interest in the woods and in the game. Youngsters and beginners can become bored with this type of hunting far more quickly than with still-hunting. On the other hand, if you've done some reading and know a bit about woods lore and various forms of wildlife, you can enjoy yourself mightily just sitting there in the quiet and becoming one with the woods. I know of no better way to regain my sense of proportion than to get away from the anthill affairs of men and spend a morning stand hunting for squirrels in the woods. Sometimes—quite often, in fact—I don't even shoot the squirrels, preferring to watch them and experiment with them. It's often fascinating to see how close they will come to you if you remain absolutely still. (On more than one occasion I have had gray squirrels come close enough for me to touch, and in one exciting instance I even had one—a brash adolescent fellow, no doubt—crawl over my foot!) This is not to attempt to turn you from squirrel hunters into squirrel watchers, but just to indicate the slower-paced but very real enjoyment built into good stand hunting for squirrels.

Either a .22 rifle or a shotgun can be used for stand hunting, but experienced squirrel hands usually prefer a .22 because of the extra sport. Often you will know about the squirrel before the squirrel is aware of you, and you can get a sitting shot. Even if you take a running shot, you have more of an edge on it, compared to the sudden startling flush of the still-hunter's jumped-up running shot.

True connoisseurs of standing for squirrels often prefer to gun for them with the diminutive .22 short round in solid point. These fellows try to get a close-in shot at a completely unaware squirrel, reasoning that the light, low-velocity round will remain in the squirrel, rather than pass through, and thus do maximum

Squirrel hunting without a dog often means sitting on a stand and waiting for them to come to you. With a scope-sighted .22 rimfire rifle this can be productive and highly sporty game getting!

damage. They try for head and shoulder shots exclusively and have the discipline to pass up long-distance shots beyond the capability of their low-powered ammunition. This is squirrel hunting at its sportiest and, many think, in its highest form. This kind of hunter is invariably a rifleman of the first order, and this is the best practice possible (in everything from patience and woodsmanship to marksmanship and discipline) for the aspiring deer hunter.

Other standers prefer the more potent .22 long rifle or .22 rimfire magnum (.22 WRF magnum) or 5mm Remington magnum. The latter two are about twice as powerful as the versatile .22 long-rifle round and cost about four times as much to shoot, cartridge for cartridge. Also, guns for them are somewhat more expensive than the low- to medium-priced standard .22 rifles. Actually, the extra power of the .22 WRF or the 5mm magnum is not necessary for squirrels and it destroys more meat. The .22 long rifle can be used in either hollow-point or solid-point version. The former has more stopping power but is also far more destructive to the meat. I prefer to use the solids.

An inexpensive rifle scope made especially for .22 rimfire rifles makes stand hunting more effective and more fun. These optics can be added to your rifle, complete with mounts, for only about $15 to $20 additional cost, and some .22s come with them included. They enable you to shoot accurately at longer range and help simulate the requirements of big game shooting, thus making the sport even more interesting. I like to sight my .22 in to be on point of aim at 50 yards. Then I can safely make shots out to about 65 or 70 yards without having to hold over the squirrel to allow for excessive bullet drop.

OUTLOOK FOR SQUIRREL HUNTING

Squirrels are, after cottontail rabbits and mourning doves, our third most popular game species, with some 25 million being harvested each year. Better yet, hunters could easily take double that amount without depleting the supply, assuming the habitat is not further reduced. It is extremely hard if not almost impossible for human hunters to overharvest these versatile and adaptable little sporting animals. Hunters rarely take more than about 10 percent of the fall population, which is only about one fourth of the number that would die anyway from natural causes before the winter young are born. Good eating, good hunting and good supply make squirrels among the tops in our small game species.

5

For More Fun, Take a Dog Squirrel Hunting!

I'd rather go squirrel hunting with Ray Lyter than anybody else I know—not only because he's been hunting them for over fifty years and knows so much about the game but also because he's discovered how to have so much fun at it.

Ray is a retired steelworker of about seventy summers who lives outside the small village of Halifax, Pennsylvania. We met through a mutual hunting buddy who knew we both appreciated the finer points of bushy-tail chasing. He kept telling me that Ray had raised it to the level of a small art form and he wasn't exaggerating much!

The extra fun comes from the fact that Ray hunts with a good squirrel dog. In recent years, interest in squirrel hunting in general seems to have declined a bit (though it is certainly still the second most popular type of small game hunting, nationwide, after rabbit hunting), and squirrel hunting with a good dog is fast becoming a lost art. I'm at a loss to explain either fact. Squirrel hunting is tops in both fun and excitement—especially if you use a dog. Furthermore, the little tree runners are terrific table fare and easy to hunt, and in many areas of the heavily hunted Midwest and East, they offer longer seasons and better gunning than their nearest competitors—cottontails, pheasants and mourning doves.

To top it all off, squirrel hunting with a dog offers ideal sport for older hunters such as Ray or for hunters with health problems or disabilities. The hunting is not arduous and requires limited and predictable amounts of walking, especially when

A successful squirrel hunter poses with his dog. Squirreling with a dog should not be diminishing, since this exciting sport is much more fun when shared with a good dog.

compared to rabbit or pheasant hunting. A hunter who knows where to look for squirrels and has a good dog to help pinpoint them can get all the sport the law allows in a few tiny three- or four-acre woodlots. Only one dog is necessary, or even desirable, for squirrel hunting. This is in sharp contrast to the two or three bird dogs often used on an upland bird hunt or the small pack of beagles most effectively used in rabbit hunting.

Since squirrel hunting with a dog always means taking running shots at a squirrel scampering through the trees or across the ground to get to a tree, it's best to wait until the leaves fall and the woods open up a bit before shifting into high gear. In my part of the country the leaves are peeling in earnest by early or mid-November in a typical year. So around the first week in November I usually receive the eagerly awaited call from Ray asking, "You ready to come get some squirrels? Looks like it's about time to get Belle out in the woods."

That's like asking if I'm ready to inherit money or if Charlie Brown is ready to pitch a no-hitter in Peanuts-land. You bet I'm ready!

A TYPICAL SQUIRREL-DOG HUNT

Our first hunt of last season will give you a pretty good idea of how we do things. Since we most often hunt the earlier rising, more active gray squirrels rather than fox squirrels, we usually like to be out in the squirrel woods just after daylight unless it's exceptionally cold and the squirrels won't be out until a bit later in the morning. Thus I crawled, whimpering piteously, out of a nice warm bed and into the chilled 3 A.M. blackness. Soon a jug of scalding hot coffee, thick enough to float the number 6 shot we like to use for this kind of hunting (unless turkey season is in and then it's number 2 or number 4), had repaired some of the damage and I headed up the darkened road to Ray's house some forty miles north.

By the time I got there my coffee jug was empty and I was wide awake. Then it was time for our season-opening chat and my first obligatory pats on the head for Belle, Ray's eight-year-old combination terrier and what-have-you squirrel dog. Ray filled me in on the squirrel outlook since—good hunter that he is—he had already done some pre-season scouting to get an idea of the best spots to try. It looked like a good squirrel crop this year, and we set off for the woods anticipating a good hunt.

Fifteen minutes later we were parking Ray's old pickup by a tiny patch of woods that hardly looked as if it could harbor a single squirrel, though Ray had assured me that at least eight were living there, based on his earlier scouting expeditions. Why so many squirrels in this small woodlot? Well, it was ideal habitat. It was near water and corn, had an ample supply of old hollow trees or trees with den cavities (usually formed when limbs had died and dropped off or been blown off, leaving rotten spots that turned into hollows in the tree trunks). The woods were mostly hardwoods, liberally sprinkled with the highly favored oak trees. All the signs were here for the knowing squirrel hunter, including the empty corn husks stolen from the nearby fields and scattered around the bases of several den trees.

Like any good hunting dog, Belle was feverishly anxious to get to hunting after a long season of inactivity. At one time Ray used to run his dogs in the off-season for fun and for practice, as many rabbit hunters do. But this caused several of them to stop barking "treed," and he feels that his repeated failure to shoot the squirrels they had put up ruined those dogs. Now he works his current squirrel dog only during the actual hunting and killing season.

We had hardly left the pickup and were only a crow hop into the small woods when Belle took off after her first squirrel. It was a perfect squirrel-chasing morning—a little damp, so that both dog and hunters could pussyfoot right up on their quarry through the silent leaves. In fact, we did surprise three of the five squirrels that we ultimately took while they were down on the ground switching trees or scrounging for food.

We had a bit of wind eddying to and fro throughout the small woodlot, so Belle didn't catch this fellow's scent until we were within a bare 50 feet. Just about the time she struck up her barking, the bushy-tail skidded up a big wild cherry tree like the seat of his pants were on fire. Before we left his house, Ray and I had flipped the old silver dollar and I had won the privilege of the first shot of the season. After that we'd alternate on our shots.

True to his kind, the squirrel had gone right to the top of the tree and hidden by circling around to the other side of the trunk and flattening himself there. Fortunately, it wasn't a hollow tree, or we would have lost him right then and there. Ray noisily circled to the other side of the big tree to drive him around my way. Although I strained my eyes until they watered in the crisp November cold, and the tree was almost bare of leaves, I couldn't spot this cagey old-timer. Then Ray shook a nearby hanging vine, slapping it hard and repeatedly against our tree so

90

that it made a loud noise well up the trunk toward the hiding squirrel. Belle was beside herself, sending up whole choruses of howling barks. All this commotion is often sufficient to drive a young squirrel out of hiding. Not this old chap, though.

We reversed our strategy and stood rock still and silent (causing Belle to become very irate and frustrated in the process). The seconds dragged by. The tension mounted. I began to wonder if the squirrel hadn't located some small hollow high in the tree that we couldn't see and thus holed up and lost himself for good. If so, we were only killing time waiting here. Belle was still quivering and agitated though, which implied that the squirrel was still out. Without such a signal from the dog, we might have abandoned the tree and let that one get away.

Finally, after what seemed an endless wait, a barely discernible motion caught my eye. A tiny tuft of the squirrel's tail was fluttering a bit in the freshening breeze, and as I stared a few more moments at the speck of motion, the outline of the squirrel began to resolve itself as he flattened against one of the topmost limbs.

Then he shifted his body slightly. Only a knife edge of his back was now visible, offering a tough shot at best. Squirrels are hard enough to kill cleanly when they're high in a tree, even with a good open shot. They're armor-plated little animals who take considerably more killing than do the various rabbits. And most shots aren't good ones in this type of hunting. The target is usually limited to various slices and slivers of the squirrel's anatomy as he flattens himself high up in a tree like this fellow, or they are hasty jump shots at a fast-moving squirrel running through the tree and partly hidden by the intervening limbs. Thus our use of high-velocity number 6 shot. I waited. Ray waited. The squirrel waited. Belle was going bananas and was sick and tired of waiting. I really wanted this first squirrel of the season to be a clean, one-shot kill. Not that I'm superstitious, mind you. But it's sure a nice way to open up the squirrel season!

The squirrel shifted again, edging perceptibly my way. Now his head and much of his back were visible as he stared down at Ray and Belle on their side of the tree. I raised my gun slowly, but he saw the flicker of motion and took off full tilt through the treetops. Squirrels may be slow on the ground but they're plenty fast when they take to the high road. I swung the gun ahead of him, and as the muzzle of the 12-gauge autoloader passed through his head, momentarily covering it, I touched off the shot without interrupting my swing. Down he tumbled, hitting the ground with that satisfying *thunk* of cleanly killed game. A good squirrel season was in store for us—I could already feel it!

Ray calmly nipped the next fellow, who was running full steam about 75 feet out and zigzagging through the trees like a swivel-hipped halfback going for the tie-breaking touchdown. A good shot it was, and one of many I've seen him make with the old Winchester Model 97 hammer-style pump gun that he'd bought for two dollars back in 1941. Since then he figures that it's taken, between him and assorted children, grandchildren and friends, something over five thousand squirrels. With it still in perfect working order, Ray feels that he's gotten his money's worth out of the old gun and it's a treasured hunting companion on all his outings.

I missed my next shot, so Ray ended up picking up three of the five bushy-tails that we took on that typical morning hunt. We have a six-squirrels-per-hunter daily limit in Pennsylvania, but Ray and I usually take no more than three apiece on the morning hunt. This leaves us plenty of good shooting for an afternoon round, following a nice long lunch break. Also, we don't like to take more than a maximum of six squirrels between us out of any one woods at a time. Sometimes we only allow ourselves one or two from a particular woodlot, depending upon how large it is, how many we've taken from it on earlier hunts and how hard it's been hunted by others. About two hours makes for a nice, bracing morning hunt and, in decent squirrel country with a competent squirrel dog, that should yield two hunters somewhere between three and six squirrels.

After the morning hunt we always retire to Ray's comfortable bungalow-style home for the ritual homemade root beer and a rehash of our morning's hunt and hunts long past. Then we clean the squirrels while they're still fresh and it's easier to do so. Then maybe a nap and a snack of hot squirrel mulligan stew before the leisurely afternoon hunt. A nice, easygoing way to spend a day!

HOW A GOOD SQUIRREL DOG HUNTS

Squirrel dogs use both noses and ears to good advantage, almost always locating their quarry by scent or sound before seeing it. As squirrel dogs get older, their hearing usually falls off first and they come to rely more on their noses for locating the quarry. A young squirrel dog will generally run a few feet in good squirrelly woods and then stop and cock his head, listening for the sounds of scurrying squirrels on dry leaves. He'll work the whole woods with his stop-and-go-and-listen technique, much as a human hunter would—except that his ears are far sharper and cover a much broader range of sounds than do his master's.

Older dogs follow the scent trails more noticeably. You can actually see the difference in their hunting styles, with the younger dog constantly stopping and starting and cocking his head, nose and ears well up off the ground to catch the faintest of sounds, while the older dog zigs and zags around, often retracing his steps with head and nose well down on the ground to unravel the maze of scent trails dotting the floor of the forest. Since hearing fails first, it is evidently a sense secondary to scent among the canines.

Another difference between older and younger squirrel dogs is that the more elderly dog usually barks more during the hunt and opens up sooner on a hot trail. (This is also generally the case with rabbit dogs and bird dogs as they age.) Incidentally, though good foxhounds peak early and usually have seen their best hunting years by the time they're five years old, and many bird dogs peak out in effectiveness by the time they're six or seven, perhaps eight years old, a good squirrel dog usually becomes better and better the older he gets. The sport tends to lend itself to close-hunting dogs rather than wide-ranging animals that scare up the squirrels too far out in front for the hunter to get a good shot or head them away toward the hollow den tree that means the end of the game.

The older he gets, the more a good squirrel dog seems to enjoy the game. This is understandable, since this type of hunting is not terribly strenuous and the dog is not required to cover large amounts of territory at high speed, as is the case with many other dog-related types of hunting. An older dog, like an older hunter, can be effective and enjoy this kind of hunting for many years—especially in smaller one- to five-acre woodlots that aren't in rough terrain and don't offer impenetrably thick cover. I've seen some of the best squirrel dogs around performing well—when matched with the right kind of hunter and hunting area—when they were over ten years old!

The most important element in the making of superior squirrel dogs, however, is not how well they locate game but how well they bark and *hold* treed once the quarry has taken refuge. This desire to bark treed is critical. Some dogs just don't seem to have this leaning. Many won't even bark once the squirrel has run up the tree and merely circle the tree a few times, almost absentmindedly, as if the squirrel had ceased to exist. (Which he probably has for this type of dog.) The hunter, if well behind the treed dog, may never know which tree the squirrel is in if the dog doesn't bark and then hold position. Also, if the dog isn't constantly circling the tree and craning his head upward with excitement, the squirrel may well change trees and be off into another portion of the woods with neither the dog nor the hunter any the wiser.

A good squirrel dog will hold treed for an hour or longer until called off by the hunter (in the case of a squirrel that has eluded the hunter by holing up safely in a hollow tree). Once called off, the dog should go back to the hunt and not continue to seek out the tree that still tantalizingly holds the now unreachable bushy-tail. Too much of a good thing can be bad, and one bad habit that some older dogs develop is the refusal to come off a treed squirrel. This kind of dog continually tries to circle back and open up on the same tree rather than locating fresh game. The only cure for this is strong and consistent discipline.

WHAT BREED IS BEST FOR SQUIRREL HUNTING?

Just about all good squirrel dogs I have seen over the years were mixed-breed animals that practically always featured a good dollop of terrier in their tangled family tree, and possibly a bit of hound here and there too. Belle is a good example of a

94

The critical requirement for a good squirrel dog like this one is that he stay interested in a treed squirrel even after losing sight of the quarry. Conversely, the good squirrel dog should be able to abandon an un-reachable treed squirrel, upon command by the hunter.

typical good squirrel dog. She only stands about 10 inches at the shoulder and, as she's getting a bit older and isn't run on game year-round, she's getting a bit portly, weighting in at 20-plus pounds even during the season. This extra weight offers no severe handicap, since dogging for squirrels isn't all that arduous, especially if the hunter doesn't turn a dog loose in woods that are extremely large.

Belle is mostly terrier mixed with a bit of hound. But I've seen some fairly weird squirrel dogs that performed quite well, ranging from chow-collie crosses to hound–bird dog crosses. Again, the main thing for a good squirreler is not any particular breed, conformation or size (though small dogs offer some advantages in being easier to feed and house) but rather that all-important eagerness to bark and *hold* treed and yet willingness to abandon a tree upon command.

WHERE AND HOW TO GET A GOOD SQUIRREL DOG

The best place by far to get a good squirrel dog is from a breeder/trainer who specializes in such dogs. It generally isn't necessary or even desirable to do all your own training, unless you've handled dogs a bit. Nor is it usually a good idea to try to pick up a dog for squirrel hunting from a general dog breeder. Some dogs show an aptitude and interest for this type of work and others don't, and the dog breeder specializing in this kind of dog will be working from dogs with proven records in this type of hunting.

Some of these breeders advertise in the major sporting magazines. This means you would probably be working long-distance if you go this route. There are some dos and don'ts to this game. First, find out very specifically and in *writing* whether the dog you are to get is "started," "part-trained" or "fully trained." And get the breeder to define just what *he* means by those terms. If you are a beginner at the game, it usually is a good idea to pay the extra money and opt for a fully trained dog, after thoroughly checking matters out and defining terms.

Ask the breeder for references, getting full names and addresses of other *recent* satisfied customers who also bought fully trained dogs. Call or write these customers to find out if their dogs were received in good health and were as represented as far as general health, hunting aptitude and training. Make sure that most or all references aren't from the breeder's own home area and thus from possibly less than objective personal friends and relatives. When checking the references, it's often a good idea to make the first contact by telephone to introduce yourself and ask for their help in furnishing you the information. After all, they are doing you a favor, and a brief personal contact (followed by a mail contact) often encourages fuller and more prompt information. You can keep your telephone costs down by phoning during the low-rate evening hours, direct-dialing station to station, working from a written outline of telephone questions to keep the conversation from wandering and limiting yourself to five or six minutes on the call by placing a watch or clock in front of you when you begin talking. When following up with a request for additional information through the mail, using a fill-in-the-blank questionnaire-type approach often saves the other person time and makes the whole operation more convenient.

Also, when dealing with the dog breeder, make sure you are buying the dog "on approval." Again, define this thoroughly. How long is the approval period? Two weeks? Thirty days? Sixty days? How much do you pay down for the dog before it is shipped? Fifty percent? If you elect to return the dog, do you get all your money back or do you lose any deposit or caution fee? Who pays for the cost of shipping the dog both ways if you are not satisfied with it? (You probably do.)

If possible, buy a local dog so that you can check it out firsthand before taking possession. Try to get an experienced squirrel-dog hunter to look at the dog with you, and ask to try the dog out in a nearby woods. You can frequently locate another squirrel-dog hunter through a local sporting-goods store, sportsman's club or veterinarian. Good squirrel dogs are generally reasonably priced (compared with some other types of fully trained hunting dogs, anyway) and you should be able to pick one up, depending upon where and how you are buying him, for about $75 for a "started" dog on up to $100 to $200 for a fully trained one. Usually a dog purchased locally is cheaper than one bought from a dealer who is advertising nationally. Someone has to pay for that advertising cost! (Obviously, most of these general comments also apply to buying a rabbit, coon, fox or predator dog.)

TRAINING YOUR OWN DOG

Though I do not recommend starting from scratch with your own squirrel dog, sometimes this is necessary. Even if not, you often must "round out" a dog you have purchased, because "fully trained" invariably never quite meets all the standards we tend to set for a good dog. Take your green dog out with a hunter who has a fully trained squirrel dog. As with rabbit dogs, there is little formal training, and much of it is accomplished by merely hunting a young dog with good aptitude alongside an older dog that is a fully trained and polished performer.

First, it's necessary to take the dog to a woods known to harbor a heavy concentration of bushy-tails. Since you won't actually be hunting squirrels to kill them, a suburban park that is practically overrun with squirrels is often a good place (if it's not against local laws). I'd try the dog out at around six to eight months in age, but even if he was a bit slow, I wouldn't give up on him entirely (if I already owned him) until he was about twelve to fifteen months old. If I was testing him "on approval," of course, my outlook and patience would be considerably different. Usually a good squirrel dog doesn't really begin to come into his own until he's about three years old (assuming he was started before he was a year old), and he doesn't really hit his prime until he's about five or six.

Take him out to see if he homes in on *squirrel* scent or if he is just running to and fro and after everything and anything. Try to jump a squirrel and see if the dog is interested in barking and holding treed on the squirrel, or if his attention wanders almost as soon as he loses sight of the squirrel after it has disappeared in the upper reaches of the tree. This is where an older, properly trained dog is vital, since he gives the green pup a guide and

98

This young squirrel hunter and his patient dog are trying to spook a stubborn squirrel out of a hollow tree. Note the big hole in the base of the tree, as well as the one the hunter is prodding. "Escape trees" like this one offer quick temporary refuge for squirrels surprised far away from their den trees.

99

something to emulate. If your pup has the makings of a good squirreler, exposure to the older dog should readily give him a rough idea of what is expected.

On the other hand, if your dog simply is not interested in holding treed, there's little beyond this exposure that you can do to provide the basic aptitude and interest. As I mentioned before, some dogs have the knack and others just don't.

KEEPING A SQUIRREL DOG

Since squirrel dogs are most often mixed breeds and smaller dogs, they are also usually hardy, robust and rather easy to keep and care for. A squirrel dog should be a good family dog, not being so large and rawboned as to be a bit bumptious and (unconsciously) rough for small children to be around.

As I mentioned earlier, if your squirrel dog is getting a bit older and/or a bit porkier, that is—within bounds—not the problem it can be with wider-ranging, harder-working bird dogs, coonhounds, or even rabbit runners. It is a particularly good idea to have your squirrel dog neutered, as this tends to make him a bit closer ranging and calmer—both of which are plus qualities in a good squirrel dog as opposed to, say, a pointer dog working wide-open country for upland birds or an aggressive retriever bringing in long-shot kills on ducks and geese that fall into frigid waters after being shot.

Because squirrel dogs are less limited by age, weight, soft footpads and various other health considerations than any other type of *hunting* dog (except possibly an overage coonhound enjoying a quiet retirement by treeing an occasional nocturnal 'possum), keeping a squirrel dog is not complex or expensive at all. An older dog, however, should be treated with basic care and consideration and not overworked. If he appears to be subject to occasional aches and pains due to aging (which you can often spot by restless sleeping, restlessness while awake, shivering due to low-grade pain, or short temper), don't hesitate to give him an aspirin or two (rolled inside a piece of lunch meat or hidden inside a piece of beef) to ease his discomfort. Have the vet check him periodically and don't overwork him—especially in cold, wet or hot weather.

GUNS FOR SQUIRREL HUNTING WITH A DOG

Rifles aren't the ticket for squirrel hunting, where the quarry is almost always moving or largely hidden from view. A good shotgun, usually using number 6 shot and with a modified choke or one of the variable chokes, is the best bet. I prefer the 12-gauge for all-around use, but a good 20-gauge will do fine, especially if it is chambered to hold the extra-power 3-inch magnum shells when needed.

Squirrels have a dense and surprisingly protective coat of fur, which in turn covers a thick and seemingly (at times) bulletproof hide. Most important of all, they are plucky little animals with an amazing amount of basic interior vitality. They take far more killing than most birds or animals of comparable size. Therefore, for most squirrel hunting with a dog I recommend that the hunter use the extra-power "high base" shotshell loadings that aren't necessary for most rabbit hunting. A modified choke, giving good killing patterns out to medium-long ranges, is a good compromise, though a full choke can be put to good use in larger open woods filled with higher trees where longer shots are the rule.

The type of shotgun is a matter of personal preference, though most squirrel hunters lean to the pumps and autoloaders rather than to the single-shot or double guns. My own preference is a good no-fads-or-frills autoloader, which with proper care will last the hunter a lifetime and still be of good use to his children.

CLOTHES FOR SQUIRREL HUNTING WITH A DOG

Silence isn't particularly necessary in this type of hunting, so the hunter isn't limited to the softer, quieter types of fabrics and weaves. A good wool or down coat for warmth during the

Winchoke tubes—
improved cylinder, modified and full chokes—
come with a handy wrench.

The tubes fit tightly into the barrel,
change quickly, and pattern right,
making the Winchoke shotgun three guns in one.

Squirrel hunting with a dog can often involve short- to medium- to long-range shots depending upon how tall the trees are in the woods being hunted. Shotguns with a built-in variable choke, such as the Winchester Models 1300 and 1500 featuring the changeable Winchoke device, make a single gun serve in any situation. (Photos courtesy of WINCHESTER-WESTERN*)*

cold of winter, topped off by a standard hunting coat with outsize pockets and game bag, is the standard garb worn by most.

Basic upland-bird-hunting-type boots will do fine, though you will find yourself around dampish, marshy bottoms more frequently than will your rabbit-hunting counterpart, so a pair of galoshes or rubber hunting boots are also a good idea. Woolen pants during winter or denims in warmer country are fine. The squirrel hunter usually won't be negotiating the prickly thickets and briars the rabbit hunter will, so that kind of protection isn't so necessary.

A FINAL TIP

Don't rely on your squirrel dog to do all the work. After all, your non-dog-using squirrel-hunting buddies must learn a bit about the biology and habitat preferences of squirrels, so do some scouting to locate them and generally stay alert to changing trends in feeding areas so that they are not wasting too much time in woods empty of squirrels.

Though your squirrel dog will give you an enormous advantage, don't rely on the dog wholly. If there are few or no squirrels in an area, your dog can't work miracles. He can only find what is there for you, not conjure up what isn't. So don't discontinue all your scouting and visiting with local farmers, landowners and game wardens. If you do stop these activities, you'll not only be lowering your bag of squirrels, you'll be losing out on some of the year-round out-of-season fun of squirrel hunting and be putting your dog and yourself through some frustrating and fruitless times afield.

6

The *Other* Squirrels

The Alaskan big game hunt had been a highly successful one, and my hides and horns had all been properly skinned, salted and packed for shipment to the taxidermist. Tomorrow the bush plane would be in to end what had been one of the most memorable and enjoyable experiences of my life. I had spent the morning getting my gear together, taking additional candid photos around camp and double-checking my trophies. Now, with the balance of the afternoon on my hands, I thought it time to do a bit of exploring. Borrowing the outfitter's ancient iron-sighted .22 rimfire rifle to try and pot a few grouse for the table, I set out with a pair of binoculars and a light lunch in my day pack.

I had earlier noted a fair amount of arctic ground squirrel activity in the valley north of camp when I had flown in two weeks earlier, and I decided to see what kind of sport I might find. As I worked my way up the broad gravel-floored valley, I carefully glassed for the telltale "picket pin" figures of the chubby little ground squirrels as they sat upright to look for danger. Also, I was constantly alert for the flicker of motion that signaled a fast-decamping rodent heading for the safety of its burrow.

Ahead of me some sixty yards out, I spotted my first target sitting there calmly surveying me. My first shot told me the old museum piece of a .22 was shooting high and considerably to the right. One shot was all each of these cherubic rodents allowed before they scampered for their nearest burrow entrance. Several more misses convinced me I'd have to ease up much closer

The black-tailed prairie dog, one of the largest and once perhaps the most numerous of the ground squirrels, sits up in the classic "picket pin" posture of all ground squirrels to look for danger. (Photo courtesy of WYOMING FISH & GAME DEPARTMENT*)*

if I wanted a squirrel or two to experiment with for the evening meal.

Most of these squirrels, even though they had been little disturbed by man, wouldn't let me get much closer than fifty yards before they broke for cover. A few did, and a couple of them finally ended up in the plastic bag in my day pack. I found it rather sporting to edge up close to the burrow of a squirrel that I had flushed and then wait patiently to see if it would reappear and how long it would take. About half of them would poke a beady-eyed head up out of the hole within ten minutes, and if I wasn't out in the open and too close to the hole, within another five minutes they had edged fully out of the burrow so I could shoot again.

All told that long afternoon I fired up more than a box of shells and pocketed half a dozen of these large ground squirrels. Later I found the meat to be dark and a bit greasy. I would not count it among the more appetizing game I've sampled, though it has over the years been a great favorite with most of the far northern Indians whom I have asked about it. Perhaps my palate is at fault or, more likely, a bit of experimenting with seasonings would improve the taste a bit. In any event, I would not rate these fellows nearly as highly for the table as I do the tree squirrels, which are quite good.

In later years I was to find that the various ground squirrels farther to the south, more used to man and his encroachments, were considerably more wary and that .22 rimfire rifles were totally inadequate for the long-range shooting required.

GROUND SQUIRRELS AS A GROUP

The ground squirrels, even after excluding the larger wood-chucks and marmots and the smaller chipmunks and pocket gophers (the latter being found in a different taxonomic order), comprise a large and varied family of animals. The nineteen species of animals range from the farthest-north tundra (arctic ground squirrel) to well down into Mexico (Mexican ground squirrel, spotted ground squirrel and roundtail ground squirrel). They range in size from the rather large arctic ground squirrel

The thirteen-lined ground squirrel, one of the smallest of the many types of ground squirrels, is a tiny target that is difficult to hit at long ranges. (Photo by Leonard Lee Rue III)

and the whitetail and blacktail prairie dogs (11 to 13 inches in body length plus stubby tails and 1½ to 3 pounds in weight) to the elfin spotted, Townsend and thirteen-lined ground squirrels, which will run only 4½ to 7 inches in body length (plus stubby tails) and a mere ¼ to ½ pound in weight.

107

At one time some of these animals, in particular the two prairie dogs, were among the most numerous animals on earth. There are many reliable estimates of prairie-dog towns containing from 5 million to (in the case of the enormous "dog town" north of San Angelo, Texas, which in 1900 encompassed an area some 100 by 250 miles) 400 million animals! These vast numbers have been systematically reduced by man because of the competition with domestic livestock for forage and the danger to both horses and livestock from the burrows or "chuckholes." But there are still many ground squirrels available for the enterprising rifleman who wants to spend time in pursuit of them. Most ranchers and landowners are only too glad to let you do a bit of "dog shooting" on their lands, after they are convinced you will close all gates and mind your safety manners when crossing fences and shooting.

Ground squirrels may be found at all elevations. The black-tailed prairie dog, for instance, prefers the lower and flatter ranges, while its somewhat smaller and less populous cousin, the white-tailed prairie dog, prefers altitudes above 6,000 feet. Some are more wary than others, depending mainly upon how much they have previously been disturbed by man. Since ground squirrels are preyed upon by just about every predator that flies or walks, however, they can be rather shy.

These animals are western and southwestern types, though the little thirteen-lined ground squirrel does range as far east as eastern Michigan and Ohio. Most of them are highly colonial animals and prefer to live in large to medium-size colonies. Some remain active year-round, while others of the Far North or those that live at higher elevations will hibernate for up to seven months of the year. Still others that dwell in the hotter and lower elevations will estivate (hibernate in the summer) for up to six months of the year during the hotter periods. Look for these types to be most active during the early and later hours of the day. All ground squirrels are diurnal, not nocturnal, animals.

HUNTING THE GROUND SQUIRREL

As with the case of the "other" rabbits (the hares and jack-rabbits) ground-squirrel hunting is more of a shooter's sport than a hunter's sport. However, in sharp contrast to hunting jackrabbits, which offers many medium to long-range running shots at flushed game, this sport often means long to ultra-long-range shots of standing game. This calls for heavy, long-barreled rifles with high-power scopes and flat-shooting cartridges.

Actually, it is possible for the sportsman to get some good ground-squirrel shooting with a deer rifle (if it is reasonably accurate and he's a deliberate shot) if he has a goodly number of prairie dogs or other ground squirrels in the area.

Flat-shooting medium to large-size game rifles such as the .270 or 30/06 can be successfully used for this type of hunting, especially if they wear a variable-power scope capable of magnification up to 7x or 9x. These guns are a bit expensive to shoot (though the costs can be reduced more than half by hand loading), and the extra muzzle blast associated with them can be a minus in some situations. But using the same gun that he will carry during the fall big game season does provide a positive benefit by keeping the hunter's shooting fine-tuned throughout the year. Hunting weight .243- , 6mm- or 25/06-caliber rifles are even better for this type of work.

However, if the shooter becomes more involved with this type of sport and wants to up his hit ratio, this invariably means using a more specialized gun such as a heavy, long-barreled .24- or .25-caliber rifle or one of the hotter-stepping .22 centerfires that will push a 45- or 50-grain bullet along at 3,300 to 3,900 feet per second. The .223, 22/250 or .220 Swift are all good choices. Since these are western targets shot in more open, windy country than the East or the Midwest, the larger .24- or .25-caliber centerfires with their heavier bullets do better at the longer ranges. Whether this is offset by their heavier recoil (still light), muzzle blast and expense to shoot is something the individual hunter will have to decide. The milder .22 centerfires, such as the classic .22 hornet or .222 Remington, are a pleasure to shoot, but they limit the sure-killing range to about 125 to 175 yards on these smallish animals.

Ground squirrels can usually be located by cruising the roads and searching for the telltale "picket pin" signs of animals standing up beside their burrow entrances, as we have seen, or by talking with local game wardens or landowners. This is

109

This young ground-squirrel hunter used a scope-sighted .22 WMR magnum for his bag of "picket pins." (Photo by Jack Atcheson, Jr.)

somewhat more specialized sport than many other branches of small game hunting, and how attractive this pastime may be for you depends upon how much emphasis you want to place on the shooting as opposed to the hunting aspects. To do well in this sport you will need to consider investing upwards of $200 to $400 for a good, super-accurate rifle and scope, depending upon whether you buy a new or used rig. It is quite possible to spend $700 to $1,000, if you really want to chase the holy grail of the "ultimate" rifle capable of tack-driving accuracy well beyond 300 yards.

PART II

The Big Game of
Small Game Hunting

7

Collecting on Coons

I don't think I'll ever forget my first coon hunt. It was some years ago in the Deep South, and I was being indoctrinated by two real pros as we huddled around the small fire for warmth in the midnight chill of late January.

"Down here in the South, Tom," mused John Campbell as he stirred our faltering fire, "we call coons *dead game*."

Through the eerie well-bottom blackness of the Alabama swamp, the dogs howled again. The hound music was coming every minute or so now. They were right behind the coon and pushing him hard. It wouldn't be long.

John Reardon, the other half of my fanatical duo of coon-hunting guides, chuckled as he adjusted his miner's light, checked his compass one last time and got ready. "Of course John doesn't mean 'dead' as in deceased or lifeless," Reardon mused. "Far from it. Coons are anything but that kind of dead. What he means is that an eight- or nine-pound coon, when he's cornered, won't hesitate to take on a whole pack of dogs. He'll try to get his back up against some place where the dogs can't get at him, like a cutbank or a big rock, or he'll go for shallow water, where he can stand up and try to drown any dogs that come at him. But wherever he's at when cornered, he'll fight till the end. He's *dead game* in the best sense of that phrase!"

Now the hounds were howling almost continuously. Suddenly the tenor changed as all six of them began baying, and even I—a novice at coon hunting—could tell they were barking treed. Both Johns checked their equipment once more, adjusted their hip boots at high mast and plunged off into the murky gloom with me right behind them. It was January, which is Alabama's rainy season, and the lowland swampy area we were hunting was pretty mushy.

The two of them plowed straight ahead, through or over anything in their path. From seemingly impenetrable honeysuckle thickets to wet sumps that tried to suck off my hip boots as I sank knee deep into them to the countless beaver ponds that run three to four feet deep in this flat country, we plowed ahead with the awful certainty of a Tiger Tank.

We were getting closer. I hung onto my little three-cell flashlight with a death grip and tried to follow the two Johns as closely as possible to take advantage of the much brighter beams thrown by their big miner's lamps. I had the feeling that I'd topple off the end of the world if I wandered too far out into that infinite blackness on all sides. Tree vines, many studded with wicked briars, clutched and tugged like claws from all sides as we pounded ahead.

Suddenly we were there. The dogs were leaping and wailing like banshees at the base of a large dead tree. The coon was clearly visible, hardly 30 feet up. As John Reardon raised his old double-barreled Fox shotgun to send a load of number 8 shot at the coon (Alabama has a large deer herd and, since hunting them illegally by jacklighting at night is a favorite avocation of some citizens, nighttime coon hunters are penalized by a law limiting them to shotguns with number 8 shot or smaller and absolutely no .22s allowed), Campbell said, "Hold on a minute."

Coons usually shinny up the biggest tree around when pressed hard by the hounds. Most of the time this is an old hollow "home tree" (or, as we call them in my Pennsylvania woods, a "den tree"). He'll either be all the way up in the stratosphere at the top of a very tall tree or, if possible, safely tucked inside a hollow. This one had made the mistake of climbing up a large tree that had been split in two by lightning and thus was actually only a 30- or 35-foot-tall stick-up. Fortunately for us, the tree hadn't been dead long enough to become hollowed out.

I could see the coon plainly, and it was obvious he was a big

114

Because of its very high intelligence, ability to learn and adapt, and omnivorous eating habits, the raccoon is undoubtedly the most destructive single predator in North America, especially since man has eliminated or greatly decreased most of its natural enemies. This doesn't mean that coons themselves should be eradicated, but in many areas they do need to be stringently controlled, and coon hunters are a big help in this respect. (Photo by Leonard Lee Rue III)

115

one, about 15 pounds, which is far larger than the 8- to 10-pound average found in these Deep South woods. Campbell had said something earlier about needing a live coon to keep for dog-training purposes (they use them to lay scent trails), since he had two raw young pups at home that needed a lot of work. He had brought along a pair of telephone lineman's spurs and a climbing belt for just such an eventuality as this.

He quickly changed boots and donned the climbing rig as the other John and I rigged up a "lasso pole" for him consisting of heavy-duty wire doubled up and run through a length of pipe to form an adjustable catch-noose at the end. Then Campbell clanked his way up the tree and gingerly swung a leg over the topmost limb. Meanwhile B'rer Coon hadn't been just sitting there woolgathering. He'd edged all the way out to the shaky end of that same top limb.

Campbell eased toward him gingerly and, after a lot of sparring and jockeying around, finally succeeded in slipping the noose over his head. Then the coon turned into a squawling, spitting, tooth-snapping little demon. John was just trying to hang on for dear life and not become airborne.

Finally, nearly an hour later, we had one very tired coon hunter safely down the tree and the coon, still not very happy about things but pretty well exhausted, safely tucked away in a large burlap bag. We stoked up a big fire to ward off the damp chill and passed around a thermos of coffee hot enough to fry our tonsils and strong enough to turn cheap jewelry green. It was also somewhat thicker than most of the surrounding watery terrain that we had been slogging through to catch our ring-tailed friend.

Coon hunting is a special kind of sport. You either like it fanatically or it leaves you cold. There is little middle ground. Basically, though coons are found in large numbers throughout almost all the contiguous forty-eight states, coon hunting is primarily a southern, eastern and midwestern sport. The Rocky Mountain and far western states, though most of them have a lot of coons around, just don't yet seem to have many people interested in hunting them. I predict that this will change considerably in the next few years.

116

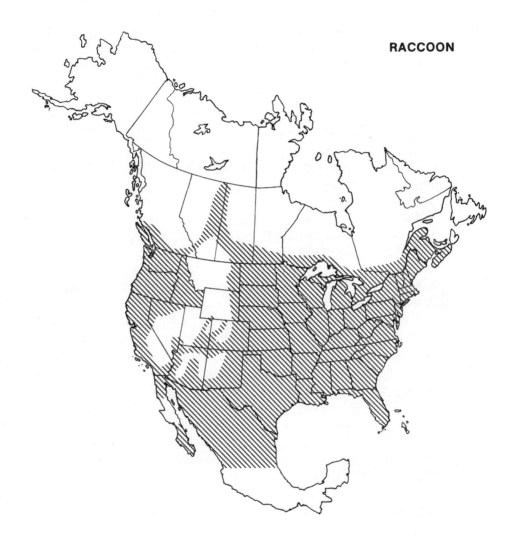

RACCOON

Coon hunting is an extended-season sport, going year-round in some southern states. (Though the killing season may be limited to a few months, the hunters can and often do get out and run their dogs throughout the year on this heavily dog-oriented sport.) It's also a fine workingman's sport in that it can generally be practiced a short distance from home, even around major population centers in many instances.

SOUTHERN VS. NORTHERN COON HUNTING

I was to find out on this hunt that southern-style coon hunting is considerably different from its northern equivalent. Although many people immediately think of such hotbeds as Ohio, Indiana, Illinois, Iowa and Michigan when thinking of coon hunting, the Southerners really take their sport equally seriously! However, where the average-sized coon may run 18 to 20 pounds in more northerly climes (one coon-hunting buddy of mine in the Finger Lakes region of New York State has caught and weighed a 28½-pounder, which is one Goliath of a *wild* coon), the coons in the Deep South usually weigh about 8 to 10 pounds. They're leaner and longer-legged and have larger woods in which to stretch those legs and run it out with the dogs. Farther to the north much of the hunting is done in scattered woodlots interspersed with farm fields. Once the coon is located and his scent trail is struck, he is frequently treed in these smaller patches of woods within five to ten minutes.

The southern races, often run in huge timber tracts owned by large paper and pulpwood companies but open to public hunting, are generally far longer. John Campbell once timed ten random races. They lasted from ten minutes for the shortest one to three hours and fifteen minutes for the longest. The average was about forty minutes. John and most of his friends were quite surprised at this. They had assumed that the average race would run over an hour. The excitement is so electric during one of the howling, baying chases that time seems to stretch out much longer.

The biggest coon either of them ever caught weighed a tad

118

The essence of coon hunting distilled into a single picture. The hounds have treed this big coon after a twenty-minute chase and will now try to hold it until the hunters can catch up with them.

more than 17 pounds, or just about average for my Pennsylvania and New York coon-hunting friends. Coon hunters in the northern states, however, suffer from some disadvantages in addition to generally shorter races. (In this dog-dominated sport, the dog music and the excitement of the race are at least half the sport.) Northern hunters lose several months of precious sport each year due to cold weather. Whenever the temperature gets much below 35 degrees Fahrenheit, the coons will go semi-dormant and den up. They won't be out and around to leave a scent trail for the dogs to follow. In Alabama, where the weather seldom stays much colder than that for extended periods, the two Johns hunt year-round, even though the killing season only runs from October through February.

October and November are the best months to coon hunt in the South and also throughout most of the rest of their range. In the South there isn't yet too much water in the low, flat country and you can still walk back into most areas. It's nice and warm then, though later (such as during our January hunt) the beaver ponds begin to fill up and it gets downright chilly. The best nights to hunt for coon are clear, moonless and crisp but not too cold. If there is a bright full moon, the coons seem to den up more often and not be stirring around. Many coon hunters believe the animals can see you too readily and know you can spot them more easily on brightly lit nights.

If it's clear enough to see all the stars, there's usually enough light for you to navigate by (after you get your night vision), and yet the coons will still probably be out stirring around. The best times to hunt them, the times when there is the most activity, is early and late during the night. In really good "coony" woods, however, there's frequently some activity all night long.

Coons usually aren't as plentiful in the South as they are in comparable woods farther north. The most single coons that John Campbell has ever caught in one night during over twenty-five years of ardent coon hunting is six. He has taken up to fourteen, counting family groups. Incidentally, in most areas, whether southern or northern, coon hunters perform a real conservation service by keeping the raccoons thinned down to balanced levels. Man has inadvertently removed most of the coons' natural enemies and they are highly intelligent and at times destructive animals that can get out of hand all too easily, with resulting detrimental effects on both other game species and on the local farmers. Coon hunters, as a group, are good conservationists who know how many animals to take and when and how many to leave for a seed crop.

COON-DOG BASICS

Dogs and their music are the heart and soul of coon hunting. Although most hunters in the area mentioned at the beginning of this chapter seem to favor Treeing Walker hounds, there are six "classic" breeds of coonhounds recognized by the United Kennel Club, and I'm not about to go into any discourse on how or why a bluetick is better than a redbone or how either compares with a Walker or one of the other coon breeds.

Good untrained pedigreed pups of any of the breeds usually go for $75 to $125, with males usually costing about $25 more than comparable bitches. A decent grown, trained hound will average around $300 to $500 in cost. John Campbell's current lead dog, Thunder, cost him $650 when the dog was three and a half years old, and within two years of intensive work after that John was offered anywhere from $1,000 to "name your own price." To my knowledge, the highest-priced field-trial national winner went for $9,500, and that was some years ago. Undoubtedly, many national champions since then would command a good bit more money.

Many owners of field-trial winners won't sell their dogs at any price since they are worth a good bit of money at stud. Also, if the dog belongs to a working coon hunter, even though most cooners are far from rich, the hunter usually figures that he can always get money some other way but a dog like this might truly be the hound of a lifetime whose like he may never see again.

Actually, it is not necessary for the beginning coon hunter to invest a lot of money in a dog to get started. The first thing to do is strike up an acquaintance with some veteran hunters who live near you. They are usually easy to locate by checking with local sporting-goods stores, hunting clubs, kennel clubs or fraternal lodges. These veterans can usually advise the beginner on when and where to pick up a good buy on a young dog. And if you have an opportunity to run your beginning dog with his pack of veteran hounds, it can make all the difference in developing both the young dog and the beginning coon hunter. Cooners are without exception friendly, outgoing types who always welcome newcomers to their ranks and try to help initiate them into the sport as painlessly as possible.

Most serious cooners like to keep four to six hounds at one time. That gives them two or three to run on Friday night, and two or three more to run on Saturday night while the first platoon is resting. Cooners usually hunt in pairs, each bringing two or three dogs. The ideal pack (if the dogs know each other and get along well together) is probably four.

Having four to six dogs at home at any one time also allows the serious coon hunter to have both mature, fully trained dogs that hunt well for him and also a pup or two always coming along to keep his pack filled out. Coonhounds usually hit their peak around four or five years of age, and they will often run well until they are seven or eight (much later than the hunting life of the harder-running foxhounds, incidentally). But good coon dogs can usually still tree well, albeit more slowly, until they're about ten years old if they are in generally good health. Many older citizens, too old themselves for the faster pace of coon hunting, like to use these older and slower dogs for the much slower-paced sport of 'possum hunting.

Although some of the very best trailing and treeing coonhounds are not good kill dogs, most dedicated coon-dog lovers feel that is necessary if the dog is to be a good all-around hunter. Although a single dog, if he's a good one, should be able to take on a coon and kill it by himself, coons don't die easy. A coon has a loose, somewhat slack hide like a badger, and it's hard for the dog to get a good grip.

When the coon comes tumbling down out of the tree, he's ready to take on all comers, and a dramatic fight almost always ensues. The coon will try to jump up on the dog's head and literally ride on his back and neck where the dog can't get at him.

122

All the while the coon is working those tremendously dextrous little hands and those long, powerful teeth. Either can cause damage, but the claws usually make only superficial wounds, while the sharp teeth can be deadly.

A good, experienced coon dog will try to get the coon between the front legs and, after grabbing him in this chest area, keep pushing the coon to the ground. The dog will, if he can, pin the coon there and eventually kill him. Some dogs are phonies. They want you to think they're brave so they'll nip at the coon's backsides while the other dogs keep him busy. If the coon turns on them, however, they'll yelp and retreat. A good aggressive dog presses in inexorably for the kill. If the coon can, when the dog has him by the chest, he will try to get his head or feet up and work on the dog's face. The dog will then shake the coon like a terrier does a rat and throw him back to earth again to try to keep him pinned. All told, it's a whirling, screeching blur of excitement when dogs and coon meet in a dramatic fight.

Interestingly enough, though coonhounds are bred to kill, few of them are ill-tempered or mean. Sure, they'll occasionally scrap a bit with each other in the pen, especially if unduly crowded or not hunted enough. (These are lean, rawboned hounds bred to hunt, not lap dogs or house pets.) And they may skirmish a bit with a strange hound, in the way of all animals, in order to establish dominance. But they are basically among the finest and most even-tempered of dogs.

NECESSARY COON-HUNTING GEAR AND EQUIPMENT

Coon hunting takes a fair amount of gear and know-how. Hunters, even in the warm Southland, wear insulated coveralls and rubber boots to protect them against the damp, all-night chill. It's easy to get cold in the early morning hours of a damp night, especially if you are sitting and listening to the hound music rather than running along after the hounds. Boots are even worn in summer, down south, in order to protect hunters from the ever-present danger of poisonous snakes. Duck jackets and overalls, lighter in weight than the insulated coveralls, are

These coon hunters have rigged up their pickup truck especially (and inexpensively) for their favorite sport. Dogs can be carried in the two separate rear compartments, comfortably floored with straw, immediately behind them, or the partition between the compartments can be removed to carry more dogs in a single large area.

usually worn in summer months. It's vital that the garments be heavy and closely woven enough to turn and shed most of the briars and stickers that are so easy to blunder into when you're tearing through the dark woods, wide open at flank speed.

A compass is always a good idea since it's twice as easy to get turned around in nighttime woods. Most hunters usually carry them securely pinned to their jacket front or lanyarded around their necks. Dog leashes are carried neatly and securely looped around their shoulders or waists so that the hunters can catch and leash their dogs as necessary.

Serious coon hunters carry powerful miner's lights, usually costing $60 and up, not including the charging apparatus. These

124

Readying his lead hound for the hunt, this hunter carries special equipment: a protective hard helmet with headlamp for night vision and an extra dog chain or leash wrapped around his chest and shoulder.

terrific lights seem made to order for coon hunting. Not only are they extremely powerful but they can be focused either into a narrow, extra-powerful spotlight beam or, by rotating the lens, into a widely diffused, softer beam that illuminates a much wider area in a softer glow.

These big lamps can run for twelve to fifteen hours on a single charge. When a coon is treed the hunter usually slips an amber disk over the light, because to spot a big coon high up in a

125

large tree it's usually necessary to get the animal to look at you in order to pick up his eyeshine. Coons will not readily look out into a bright light. In fact, the old-time cooners used the temperamental, at times downright dangerous carbide lamps that miners of an earlier era were cursed with. These lamps, along with old kerosene types that were sometimes used, would throw only 20- to 25-foot beams, but that would often make the coon look your way.

Even today, sometimes, if veteran coon hunters can't spot a ringtail they know is up a certain tree, they'll douse all the lights and build a small pine-knot fire (where legal) at the base of the tree. This often seems to pique the creature's curiosity and he will peer down, giving himself away with those shiny, beady eyes.

Another way to locate difficult coons is to use a mouth squawler—another handy piece of gear. This is blown like a duck or predator call, and there are a number of commercially made types available, though some hunters delight in making their own and are continually experimenting in order to improve the pitch or tone of their favorites. No one knows exactly why this technique often works when nothing else will. The squawler more or less imitates two fighting coons (or a single squawling coon). Many times this not only makes the coon look to see what is going on (out of curiosity, I guess) but also causes him to slink down out of the tree. (Perhaps he thinks he can sneak away in all the "confusion.")

Actually, not much else is needed except a tolerant wife. A vehicle that can get into and out of the woods is handy, as is one that can easily carry several dog cages (such as an old station wagon or pickup). Much coon hunting is done from secondary roads, however, and an expensive four-wheel-drive vehicle isn't necessary at all.

GUNS FOR COON HUNTING

Fancy guns are not necessary for coon hunting. Though coons are large animals by small game hunting standards, and can absorb punishment out of proportion to their size, the way they are hunted implies straightforward armament. Anything that will knock them out of the tree will do fine. Many hunters prefer a simple .22 with iron sights, an inexpensive gun that they

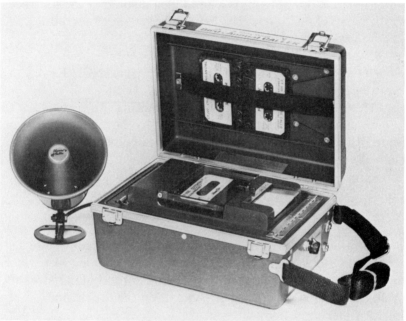

A coon squaller (top) is used not so much to call coons in to the hunter as to make them (for reasons no one quite understands) come down when treed. These are inexpensive items, and every coon hunter should have at least one.

Of the various electronic calls available for raccoon and other predator calling, the cassette type seems best, being lighter and easier to use at night than record players; and they broadcast farther and stand up better to hard field use than "homemade" kinds employing cheap drugstore-type players. (Photos courtesy of Johnny Stewart Game Calls, Waco, Texas) don't have to worry about scratching or otherwise distressing by rough handling. Remember, this sport is far more of a *dog* sport and a *hunting* sport than it is a shooting sport.

Some hunters do use shotguns and, though opinions vary depending upon how large the coons run and what size trees and woodlots they are most often taken in, preferred shot usually ranges from number 2 through about number 6, unless there is some law on the books (as in Alabama) restricting the hunter to very small shot sizes because night poachers are also afield. Again, a simple and inexpensive scatter-gun is called for. A sling, for either rifle or shotgun, is a good idea if some of the footraces to the treed coons tend to be long and over rough terrain.

HOW TO LOCATE GOOD COON-HUNTING AREAS

The best way to find good coon-hunting areas is to get to know veteran coon hunters and learn by hunting with them. State fish and game department offices can be helpful too, especially if you get the name of the local game warden or biologist in your area who is personally acquainted with local field conditions. Also, you can check at the local sporting-goods store for advice.

Perhaps the most rewarding method of all is to locate your own hunting areas. You can do this by cruising back roads during the day to look for coon tracks and sign. Coons like water, and they usually live near it and forage for food along streams. Walk these small ponds and streams, even the tiniest ones, looking for fresh coon tracks.

Another good idea is to check nearby cornfields and gardens or other fields near water. When a coon has been raiding a cornfield, the signs are unmistakable. If squirrels or other corn-nappers have been feeding on the corn, the partially eaten ears will often still be on the stalk; even if the ear has been pulled off, the stalks will be unbroken in most cases. Coons invariably climb a cornstalk, bend it over with their ample weight, and stand on the ground and eat the corn. Or the coon might take the ear out of the husk (those dextrous monkeylike hands again) and

128

move off toward the nearby stream to eat it. Either way, when coons have been raiding cornfields, the stalks are bent and broken.

Coons also eat acorns, beech mast, crayfish and frogs. They dearly love soybeans and watermelons. In fact, they are among our more omnivorous animals. When running coons in the summer (though not killing them), hunters should always check any watermelon patches encountered, because if there are coons around they will be drawn to the big melons like a magnet. The way coons eat melons is as interesting as it is unique. A coon will hollow out a round hole in the side of a melon, about the size of a silver dollar, and then stick his hand into the melon and clean it out as neatly as if it were eaten by a fastidious person with a spoon. And he'll do it all without ever breaking open the melon.

THE PECULIAR EXCITEMENTS OF COON HUNTING

Coon hunting is for dog lovers. A man who likes dogs, likes to keep them and work with them, is usually a good prospect for coon hunting. Most coon hunters are one-sport men because not only can they hunt for most or all of the year (or at least run their dogs that long), they truly work at it year-round, considering all the dog training and utility dog work necessary. It's not a terribly expensive sport as recreation goes, either, and the dedicated cooner will usually be out three or four nights a week during the height of hunting season (though that may mean he is occasionally a bit sleepy-eyed at work the next day).

Coon hunting is also a companionship sport. Practically no one hunts alone, since one of the major joys is sharing the fun and excitement with others around the campfire, plus the friendly rivalry in figuring out whose dog is in the lead most often during each race as the dogs hit the scent of a coon and shift into high gear to run him down.

The quarry is an interesting and intelligent animal that is plentiful and should be for years to come, since it is adaptable and seems to thrive on the edges of civilization.

Good trophies can be taken from coons. The small skulls can be saved, boiled in sal soda (see chapter 16, on trophies) and

These hunters have captured their coon alive in order to keep him for training their younger dogs, by laying scent trails for them to follow. Many times coon hunters, in hard-hunted areas, will call their dogs off and leave the quarry to run another day. Coon hunters are good conservationists. The last *thing they want to do is to run out of coons!*

bleached with peroxide if desired, for an interesting paperweight or piece of bric-a-brac. The pelts, when good winter fur, make lovely little rugs that can be inexpensively tanned by a taxidermist or tannery into luxurious wall hangings or small throws to go over the backs of chairs or couches. Some dedicated cooners even have their first coon or perhaps a particularly big one mounted whole as the centerpiece for a mantel or bookshelf.

Coon hunting is not for everyone, but it is my feeling that every good, well-rounded small game hunter and general outdoorsman should give it a try. It's easy to become addicted to coon-dog music. There's something about it that makes the hackles rise on the back of your neck when you're cozied up to a warm, crackling fire with a few buddies on a cold night. Try it sometime!

130

8

Cornering the Coyote

Hunkered down in the sagebrush of the rolling Wyoming prairie, I waited patiently, hoping the enormous mule-deer buck we had seen twice in that area would wander by. It was a bit of a long shot, but well worth it for that gigantic rack. Dusk was falling, and here at this 7,200-foot altitude it was quite cold. Fine snow began misting down as I caught a flicker of motion well out to my left. There it came again. Something was coming through the high sagebrush and crossing at an angle about 130 yards in front of me.

Trying to quit my shivering, I raised the 8x binoculars and trained them on the object flitting almost ghostlike through the darkening clumps. A coyote—the first wild one I had ever seen and a relatively rare sight in this area. (This was some years back during the height of the poisoning and other means used in this period of all-out, unrestricted warfare on the little wolves.) The animal loped closer, without an idea in the world that I was anywhere around.

I debated whether to try for him and ruin my chances at the big mule deer. The rapid darkening of the sky and another hasty look at the long prime early-winter fur worn by the animal convinced me that this was a fine little trophy in its own right and well worth trying for. I raised the .270 and tracked along with the moving target. I brought the muzzle in front of his nose as he moved through a small clearing and touched off the gun. The animal suddenly seemed to disappear as if magically erased from the scene.

131

Sure that I had missed, I stood up to scan the area for another chance at the rapidly departing brush wolf. Nothing. Even the binoculars did not reveal the slightest sign of life. Hastily I picked my way over to the clearing in the rapidly fading light. There, about 10 feet from where I had last seen him, lay my trophy—a beautifully furred little wolf with extra-heavy, long winter fur sprinkled with black-tipped guard hairs—shot cleanly through the head.

Thanking the hunter's gods for what was mostly a lucky shot, I shouldered my trophy and headed back toward the ranch house some two miles away. This was a larger-than-average coyote weighing a good 35 pounds. Fortunately, most of my trek back was downhill, because by the time I finally got there he must have weighed at least 235 pounds! I had him made into a lovely little rug with a full open-mouth head mount, and he hangs on the wall in front of me as I write this. Today that striking rug, edged all around with its blue and brown scalloped rims of felt, is as dear to me as the 16-inch pronghorn I took on the same trip—valued in a different but equivalent way.

Over a decade later and fifteen hundred miles to the southeast, game-call maker Johnny Stewart of Waco, Texas, and I set up shop in a parched, frying-pan-hot spot within shouting distance of the Mexican border. Johnny positioned himself *inside* a clump of prickly pear to break up his outline and then draped himself with camouflage cloth in an added effort to con our sharp-eyed quarry. This was a photos-only jaunt, so I set up my camera with a 50–300mm zoom lens (1x to 6x) on a tripod and draped more camo netting around it and myself. Just as I settled in, Johnny started making a plaintive, rabbit-in-distress bleat with his mouth caller. Hardly the third bleat had come out of the caller, while I was still settling in, when a big coyote exploded into view almost literally in our laps!

I don't know who was more surprised, and though it was a tense moment at the time, in retrospect it borders on the hilarious. The stringy, summer-furred animal came running out of the brush about ten feet from Johnny and hardly twenty feet from me. He heard my motor-driven camera, looked first my way and then Johnny's, and decided he'd better head out of there straightaway and figure things out later in safer surroundings. If it's possible for an animal to convey a look of perplexity, chagrin and fright at one and the same time, this fellow tried. If we had been gun hunting I could have killed him easily, but the pictures were more fun to get, and a moment after he had left and Johnny and I had recovered our wits, we broke up in laughter. You just never know what will happen when going after these highly intelligent and curious and always exciting animals.

GETTING TO KNOW THE COYOTE

The first thing to know about coyotes is that they are endlessly fascinating. Johnny Stewart, who has spent a quarter century calling up and hunting coyotes, bobcats and foxes, says that in intelligence the coyote compares to the other two in about the same fashion that a college graduate compares to elementary school dropouts. Not a bad accolade when you consider that foxes and bobcats are themselves two of the craftiest and wariest animals on the continent!

Coyotes belong to the same family as dogs, wolves, jackals and foxes. In fact, they are the smallest of our true wolves, exceeded in size by the nearly extinct red wolf and by the much larger gray wolf, which is now largely restricted to the Far North. Where the big gray wolf has been constantly driven back and exterminated from most of its original range, the coyote (with at least the same amount of persecution by man) has been able not only to hold its own but also to extend both its geographic range and its numbers—some accomplishment in this era!

Coyotes resemble medium-sized dogs, though their muzzles are more pointed, their feet smaller and their general build a bit slimmer and racier. Despite all stories to the contrary, the coyote averages 23 to 25 pounds in weight, with the males running about 2 or 3 pounds heavier than the females. The largest coyote on record weighed some 74 pounds (killed in Wyoming in 1937) and though a few outsize specimens have been taken that weighed between 40 and 60 pounds, it's a rare animal indeed that approaches 40 pounds in the wild. By comparison, adult red wolves will run between 50 and 75 pounds in weight and the big grays will scale from 75 to as much as 175 pounds in a few instances.

Coyotes are probably the most intelligent wild animal in North America, and they are undoubtedly the most successful large predator. Their coloration is basically light buff-gray, with animals living in more thickly timbered areas and higher elevations running to the darkish side and those living in more open bottomlands tending toward a lighter gray dusted with more reddish or buff. They stand about 2 feet high at the shoulder and, including their handsome bushy tail of 11 to 16 inches in length, they are about 4 feet long. They do not hibernate, no matter how far north or how cold the area, but remain active year-round. They are tough, resourceful animals that for their size take a lot of killing.

Their Latin name, *Canis latrans,* means "barking dog" and indicates their well-known tendency to howl a lot in the wild. Though there is strong evidence to suggest that the coyote prefers open, brushy lowlands (and thus is sometimes called the "brush wolf"), probably the main secret of his success is that he will move into any area where there is ample food, regardless of the habitat. There is a saying, "Coyotes will eat anything that won't eat them," and it's basically true. They now range from Point Barrow, Alaska, at the bleak northernmost part of the continent, to Costa Rica in Central America, an enormous north-south spread of 7,500 miles. Not bad for an animal that was originally almost exclusively a desert and open-plains dweller!

This series of pictures, shot especially for this book, shows a classic coyote-calling situation. In the first photo the curious coyote has been lured (in broad daylight) within six feet to champion caller Johnny Stewart and has just looked up toward the slight noise made by the author's motor-driven 35mm camera. The next picture shows that first startled jump when the little wolf figures something is amiss, and the last indicates he is hitting top speed without sticking around to figure out just what is going on around there. This is the way it is, except that a gun is substituted for the camera in most instances.

134

135

This remarkable spread of the animal is due to the movement southward and northward of man and his livestock, with the coyote following this ready food supply, and also to the extermination (by man) of larger competitive carnivores such as the bigger wolves and the cougar. The coyote, however, has successfully colonized Alaska within the last sixty years, and there are still a considerable number of the big gray wolves up there, so he is also obviously able to hold his own even when the bigger predator is present. He can do this because of an omnivorous appetite, a keen intelligence and an apparent ability to reason out new situations almost unmatched among nonprimates.

Coyotes eat a considerable number of grasshoppers, mice and voles as well as carrion, rabbits, livestock and deer. They like to hunt around watercourses because these are natural magnets for other game, especially during dry or hot weather. In the winter, larger-hoofed animals such as deer and even young elk or caribou are helpless if a coyote can catch them trying to cross the ice or if several coyotes (they often team up to hunt together) can haze the larger prey animal out onto the ice. It's then an easy matter for them to pull down the slipping and sliding hoofed mammal, which can hardly maintain its balance, much less run or fight effectively on the ice.

Another instance that reflects the coyote's intelligence and ability to hunt together, using water, was once related to me by Jack Atcheson, the Butte, Montana, hunting consultant and taxidermist. Five coyotes (probably a bitch with four large ten- or eleven-month-old offspring) succeeded in driving an adult cow elk, a large, strong animal weighing over 300 pounds and in good health, into the Yellowstone River in a small pocket. There they held her, working in relays, in hock-deep water. They would not let her escape to either bank. After several days she weakened, and when finally, in desperation, she tried to break out, they pulled her down easily. This unorthodox strategy often might not work, but the fact that it did in this one authenticated instance demonstrates an almost matchless reasoning ability.

Coyotes provide exciting sport and make fine trophies if one turns a well-furred pelt into a nice rug. The small skull can also be kept and bleached for an interesting paperweight or shelf

COYOTE

piece. I am told coyotes are not particularly good to eat, but I've never tried one. They are hunted not as a meat animal but as a challenging trophy animal, and no sportsman has to worry about overharvesting this wily little wolf! When you win in a battle of wits with one of these fellows, you have met and conquered the best!

HUNTING THE COYOTE

Opportunistic Hunting

Probably more coyotes are shot by sportsmen as a "take 'em as they come" bonus to big game hunting (like my first one during that Wyoming deer and pronghorn hunt) than in any other way. However, there are things you can do to up your odds greatly and keep this kind of hunting from being purely a matter of chance.

The coyote usually spends most of his waking hours moving around in search of food. He prefers to hunt in the late evening, at night and during the early morning hours. Most daylight time is passed laid up in some hidden alcove where he has a good view of the surrounding country and where his back is to something, whether it be a rock bluff, a large overturned tree or stump or a single huge boulder. He usually likes to get a little elevation so he can see better over foliage that is taller than he is, and he will most often watch his back trail, facing the direction of the prevailing wind. Days after full-moon nights are not good coyote-hunting times. Chances are the coyotes have hunted and fed well in the evening hours. Low-light nights mean better dawn and evening hunting, especially if the nights have been severely cold.

Each coyote has his own runway or consistently used hunting route. Depending upon the country this will usually be some 10 to 15 miles in length. (Gray wolves and cougars pursue a similar pattern but these two larger animals may have a runway which they check completely in one night's time that stretches 50 to 75 miles and more!) With a bit of practice, it's not too difficult to dope out likely pathways in good coyote country.

These runways will usually follow along beside primary wa-

138

terways, streams and smallish rivers for a portion of the round and then take to prominent terrain features such as the spines of ridges. New snow provides an excellent opportunity for you to get out early and learn more about the coyote runways in your area. Follow those tracks from earliest light—the time spent will stand you in good stead on the hunts to come, whether you bag a coyote on that day or not. Coyotes tend to use the same hunting routes once they have proven productive. Even if you shoot a coyote off a prime hunting route, once his "signposts" (marked with urine and scratching) have had a chance to age so that the runway is declared "open," another coyote will usually move in. Good hunting routes don't change unless there is some major upheaval in the area that completely rearranges the movement patterns of the prey species being hunted.

The abundance of food, or lack of it, determines whether a coyote will leave his runway for another area. If there is adequate food, he may continue to use the same circuit throughout his entire life. He knows every nook and cranny of his territory—where to hunt and where to hide, where to drink and where to wait in ambush for prey. Why should he leave? If you surprise a coyote in one area and miss him, let that spot cool for a few weeks. Then check it out again, trying to dope out the coyote's probable feeding runway as you do so. He'll still be around and you just may catch him.

Modern highways or even well-traveled secondary routes are—believe it or not—good areas to locate coyotes, especially in the winter when times are lean and road-killed carrion is a welcome bonus. When winter begins turning to spring, the ground adjacent to paved roads warms first, due to the heat absorbed and radiated by the pavement. This means that the first shoots of tender new vegetation often spring up along the roads. This greenery draws grasshoppers and other insects (which coyotes feed readily upon when necessary), as well as rabbits, voles and other herbage-eating prey species. So when you're trying to locate good coyote hunting grounds, check those highways early and late in the mornings and evenings.

A final tip for opportunistic coyote shooting is to *watch for them,* especially in good rabbit or sheep country. Don't be surprised by them. When you are searching for other game, look for telltale coyote signs, from tracks to old kills to parts of rapidly disappearing animals. Use those magic hunter signposts—fresh tracking snow and dampish-to-wet mud and sand along watercourses—that faithfully record what has passed there. Any time spent in hunting country is productive, *if* the hunter is alert and learning every moment!

If there are any large pieces of carrion such as dead livestock or horses or big game animals in the area, make it a point to check them out carefully, especially in the winter when other food is doubly scarce. You just might get lucky. Though coyotes eat almost anything that's digestible and some things that aren't, in the winter nearly 40 percent of their diet (according to one broad-based study of nearly ten thousand coyotes) is comprised of carrion. In the summer their diet tends to be more balanced, owing to the abundance of rodents and the fact that sheep and goats (as well as big game animals) have their young. In the fall as the weather turns cooler, the percentage of carrion in the diet increases, while the rodents, larger game young and insects begin to decrease. Winter is the season of both the rabbit and of winter- and highway-killed carrion (also isolated garbage dumps). In the spring, rabbits are the main food, because of their exploding populations, and good rabbit country is the place to hunt.

Calling for Coyotes

Calling for coyotes has many similarities to calling for bobcats and foxes (as we'll discover in the next two chapters), but there are some differences in technique and degree. First, some general rules about almost all predator calling:

1. *It isn't so "deadly" as to be nonsporting.* There are no guarantees when calling game. It can work phenomenally well—*once*—in an area that has never been called. After an area has been worked, it is a good idea to rest it for three months; six would be better. If an area is repeatedly called, forget it. Coyotes are simply too smart to be fooled by the same technique frequently.

2. *Both mouth and electronic calls have their advantages.* Mouth calls are more adaptable, and pitch, frequency and—to a degree—tone can be infinitely varied as the need demands. Electronic calls, though somewhat controllable if the volume switch is "worked" (as it should be), are less flexible. On the other hand, mouth calls can become very tiring during the course of a long day's hunt. Also, good cassette callers are actual recordings of the animals (usually a jackrabbit or cottontail) squealing in distress and thus are more realistic than the sounds of a beginner with a mouth call.

3. *Know the areas you are calling.* Know how much the areas have been called before. Know whether they harbor good coyote populations. Know if you are on or near a coyote runway. Determine this by talking to the landowner when securing permission to hunt and by scouting around the area for signs on days that don't yield any game in the bag. Game brought to bag is the result of a *process* whereby hunters have learned their hunting grounds over a period of time—done their homework, if you will—and not just a random bit of luck based on plopping down here, there and yon at random with a caller, especially with crafty, hard-to-get animals like the coyote. Don't just run around trying to call strange ground because it looks "wild." Good coyote hunting can often be surprisingly close to the edge of ranches, farms or even small villages or dumps.

4. *Allow the right amount of time at each calling station.* Johnny Stewart usually figures about fifteen minutes (which is longer than it may sound here) in good coyote country, less in marginal country. It is even possible to lure two separate coyotes up during the same calling session without moving, so don't always jump up immediately after the first one comes (unless you get a shot at him). The noise of a high-powered rifle pretty well means closing up shop for that calling stand.

5. *Camouflage yourself well.* Sit with your back to some large object that will break up your outline and keep something from literally running right over you. The biggest problem with

When setting up a calling station for the sharp-eyed coyote (or other eagle-eyed predator) always try to take advantage of a position that offers *you* adequate natural concealment on the sides as well as the rear. If this is not possible, construct a temporary blind with good side concealment such as veteran game-call maker and World Champion Predator Caller Johnny Stewart has done here with camo netting.

Before leaving any calling stand, always pick up the speaker and turn it this way and that, "broadcasting" at higher volumes as a last-ditch try.

142

effective calling is just that—the game may appear from immediately behind you and be gone in a trice before even the quickest-witted hunter can react. Use camo netting generously to drape over yourself and especially over anything metallic (cameras, guns, electronic callers) that may glint in sunlight. The idea of this camouflaging routine is not to hide yourself so the animal simply can't see you—that's not possible—but to break up your outline and hide your man-made glints (the most unnatural of sights) *long enough* to allow you to recover from the surprise of an animal's coming to call and then to get off a shot before he gets away. You don't have to fool him long, just for those critical few seconds that make all the difference.

6. *If using an electronic caller, get an extension cord in order to place the speaker farther from you.* Quite possibly the biggest single advantage of the electronic caller is that the speaker can be placed away from the hunter. *Remember, the animal is coming to the sound, not to you.* In the case of mouth calling, they happen to be one and the same. For some intriguing reason, most electronic callers do not come with long cords separating speaker from player, and some don't even furnish extension cords as an extra-cost option. Try to get that speaker from 25 to 50 feet away from you as you man the player.

I have seen some fascinating situations where even coyotes, much less foxes and bobcats, have been duped into coming to the speaker and, not alarmed by the caller sitting well away from them, have circled the speaker warily, even coming up and smelling it and touching it with an extended paw. Camouflage the speaker with netting or by spray painting with dull-finish browns and greens. Most caller speakers are a neutral-toned gray color, but almost all seem to have a gleaming enamel-type finish rather than a preferred dull "Parkerized" type.

These general rules apply, to one degree or another, for almost all predator calling. When calling coyotes, keep in mind that these animals are generally the fastest reacting and most curious of the major predators, even though they are more intelligent animals than the gray and red foxes and the bobcat. This means that you should be completely ready before you ever let the first call out. Coyotes can sometimes respond within thirty seconds if they're nearby and hungry! A coyote either comes at a run or he doesn't fall for your scheme—exactly the opposite of the slower, more cautious bobcat.

Stay alert while calling coyotes. They can come, and come at a lightning-fast lope, at any time. Face away from the wind but swivel your head around periodically so that you can catch motion coming from any quarter. Stay alert for animals coming from behind you.

It's not at all unusual for a big coyote to come barreling out from behind the startled caller, take a quick look around and, without pausing, keep going, cutting right across the shocked hunter's front yard (so to speak). It can all happen so quickly that you never even get your gun up. *Stay alert!* Weird things happen when calling coyotes as compared to the somewhat more deliberate foxes and the much more deliberate bobcat. Coyotes can sometimes be called right up into the lap of the astonished novice caller, especially in areas where they haven't been called before. Stay alert also to that half of the world behind you where the wind is coming from. Even though coyotes will normally come into the wind, wind currents and eddies can be unpredictable things at best, especially on hot, still days where there is little or no direct wind and the rising thermals play hob with normal wind (and thus scent-laying) patterns.

GUNS FOR COYOTE HUNTING

Coyotes have a lot of vitality and take some killing. Also, since some shots are often taken at running animals at quite a long range, a relatively powerful and flat-shooting scope and rifle combination is recommended for all-around use. The more powerful .22 centerfires such as the 22/250 and .220 Swift will do, but I prefer the various .24-, 6mm-, .25-caliber "mediums." They kill cleaner and buck the wind better, and they offer a good combination gun for fall big game hunting for animals up to the size of caribou.

A scope is absolutely necessary for this sort of precision shooting. A fixed 4x will do, but one of the better-quality extra-wide-field-of-view 2x-to-7x variable powers is even better. The gun should have a handy carrying sling and should be capable of accuracy approaching a minute of an angle (1 inch at 100 yards), though that exact level of accuracy isn't mandatory. If the coyote hunter can consistently keep a *three*-shot group within 1½ inches at 100 yards, he's in business. (He's not often going to fire the full-scale five-shot group at running game!) Actually, the problem is usually the hunter rather than the gun if there is a lack of adequate accuracy. Most good-quality factory guns, with a bit of tinkering and shooting—possibly tightening up or backing off on the screw in the fore-end of the stock, or shimming up the barrel with a thickness or two of thin card stock between the barrel and the fore-end, or trying different factory or handloaded ammunition—will usually yield all the accuracy the average hunter is capable of under field conditions and then some.

Quality, not quantity, is the tone of coyote hunting. The bag is never large, and sometimes the trophies are depressingly few and far between. This is sport for the advanced small game hunter. Here you polish and hone your knowledge of woods lore and animal behavior. You become a student again, but of a more advanced quarry, and each victory, however infrequent, becomes more satisfying.

9

Outfoxing the Foxes

Even though we were well into the warm season, it was chilly as we waited in the midnight blackness of central Texas. Tony turned the squealing-rabbit call up a bit in volume and then flicked on the powerful spotlight. He pointed it upward at a 45-degree angle, so that a soft halo of light was thrown outward well over a hundred feet, and slowly began a sweep to illuminate the area all around us. Sure enough, we spotted eyeshine at the outer edge, but a moment later we saw that it was a chunky coon coming to investigate. That added another species to the white-tailed deer, opossum, skunk and wandering dog that we had already seen during earlier sweeps of the light. But foxes were the game we wanted.

We had been at this spot some fifteen minutes, so we decided to close down. After a twenty-minute ride down the narrow, winding back road we stopped again. We walked into the brush a couple of hundred yards to a spot that had been productive before, climbed to the top of the only small knoll in the area (for better visibility) and set out the caller again, placing the speaker about 40 feet away from our position. Then we carefully burrowed out some comfortable spots in the edge of the brush to break up our outlines, even though it was a dark-of-the-moon night. Dabbing a bit of skunk scent around helped a bit, since there was a gentle, gusting breeze—not the best of conditions for game as nose-sensitive as the fox.

This time we took a leaf from the coon-hunter's journal and snapped an amber disk over the spotlight to mute the harsh effect of the light still further. Tony started a few low, tentative rabbit squeaks with his mouth caller, and I flipped the light on. Next he hit the electronic caller, still low in volume so as not to frighten any game that happened to be nearby. A pair of eyes moved slowly into view at the very edge of the skyward-pointed light and I strained to see, hoping it was a fox rather than one of a number of other curious creatures. (When calling at night you never know what you're going to come up with!)

Then I spotted the unmistakable salt-and-pepper-gray animal with the rusty-washed flanks that meant gray fox. Though both red and gray foxes inhabited the area, this open, brushy locale was classic gray-fox territory and marginal for his red cousin. I had hoped to see a crafty red but was happy enough to see the gray. Tony lowered the volume of the electronic caller still further, muting the quavering, tremulous rabbit call to a very low pitch to coax the curious animal in. Slowly I eased the little scope-sighted .222 forward, and as the fox trotted into the 4x scope's field of view I squeezed off a shot. The bullet took him fair in the chest, a clean kill with the little trophy never knowing what hit him. Though we worked on into the early morning hours, calling from several more stations, that was our only fox. But we did call up and see over a score of animals of half a dozen species, so the evening was never dull, with or without foxes in attendance.

Though there are several North American foxes, the swift fox, the kit fox (considered by many authorities to be merely a subspecies of the swift fox) and the arctic fox are of no real significance to large numbers of American small game hunters. But the gray fox and the red fox are. Because of some fairly distinctive differences between the two, it's best that we review them in some detail separately.

THE RED FOX

The red fox is fully as sly and cunning as all the nicknames and anecdotes about "foxy" imply. Probably only the coyote

Here a crafty but completely duped red fox approaches the hidden speaker of an electronic call. Note the back of the partially camouflaged and motionless caller to the left. Foxes are easier to call in than coyotes.

surpasses it in intelligence and reasoning ability among North American mammals, though the bobcat is just as wary and considerably more deliberate. Red foxes are rangy, delicately built animals that are surprisingly slight, minus their long, flowing pelt. An adult runs 3 to 3½ feet in length, of which a foot or more is that magnificent bushy tail. They have a scent gland on the upper portion of the tail, and sometimes during the mating season or when they are particularly alarmed they can give off a pungent aroma almost as musky as that of a skunk (though not nearly as distasteful). They are far and away the muskiest of all the foxes and wolves.

An adult red fox stands about 15 to 16 inches at the shoulder and weighs from 6 to 15 pounds, though it takes a big one indeed to scale in at more than 12 pounds. The red fox is basically a

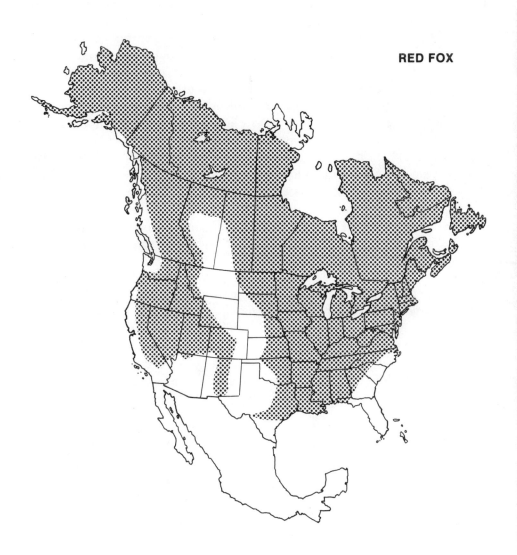

RED FOX

northern animal that has in recent times extended its range much farther south. When I was growing up in Alabama some thirty years ago, reds were unheard of. Now they are relatively common. There is considerable variation among individuals throughout this range, but the animal is usually larger and redder in the Far North and smaller and more buffy-red farther south. I have never seen a red fox in the "southern forty-eight" quite match the crimson glory of a full-furred Alaskan animal.

The so-called silver fox, once a craze in the fur business before mink ranching became quite so rationalized, is nothing but a black-color phase of the basic red fox. These "silvers" are gloriously beautiful animals and tend to run a trifle larger in size. The silver in their name comes from the grizzled or silver appearance of the long white-tipped guard hairs against the basic black pelage. They are quite rare in most locales. Some black foxes don't have the guard hairs tipped with white and thus are simply black rather than "silver."

Foxes, as one might imagine from their smaller size, restrict themselves to an average range of about a square mile or so, rather than the ten square miles or more often claimed by a coyote. They also tend to use and reuse the same basic hunting route or runway, like a coyote, but whereas the larger animal's runway is often about ten miles in length, a red fox's will average five miles or less. Foxes, like most predators, are rather nocturnal—especially in civilized areas well populated by man. But I have seen a fair number of these animals out and around during the day in Mount McKinley National Park in central Alaska. These intelligent, highly adaptable animals have learned they have nothing to fear from man in this area. I once had one come up and gaze at his reflection and sniff the hubcap of my rear tire, while I sat in the car some eight feet away with the car door open and watched. He finally hiked his leg and urinated on the tire before moving off without so much as a backward glance at me or the vehicle!

Meadow mice are the foxes' primary food, though they take a good many rabbits and some game birds, particularly the young. They also eat large numbers of beetles, grasshoppers and crickets during the insect season, as well as berries, fruits, melons and corn. Though foxes are, on balance, beneficial to man, they do show a strong penchant for poultry. They will also take carrion readily, especially during the hard times of winter.

Like all the canids, or doglike predators, smell is the red fox's keenest sense, followed probably by hearing, though it certainly does hunt by sight on some occasions. All the senses are sharp and, perhaps equally important, they are backed up by an alert intelligence that readily interprets and reacts to these senses. Again, in common with most canids, the red is not a particularly fast animal, with a top speed of about 26 miles per hour—or barely more than the faster-turning but somewhat slower cottontail rabbit. However, as with wolves and jackals, foxes are made for endurance, and they can lope along tirelessly for endless miles. This is what makes them such keen sport for the "hunters" who pursue them with specially bred foxhounds.

Though wolves, coyotes and lynx will kill foxes if given an opportunity, their biggest enemies are probably the automobile and such parasites and diseases as roundworms, tapeworms, distemper and rabies. Hunting by man has no appreciable effect on their numbers, though trapping occasionally does.

THE GRAY FOX

The gray fox is a smaller, somewhat less intelligent and more catlike animal than the red fox. Though it stands about the same height at the shoulder and is about the same length, it will weigh some 3 to 5 pounds less and thus is more lightly built. It carries the same sharply chiseled, highly intelligent face as the red, but the coat is considerably shorter and more bristly; though attractive, it has never been in demand as a fur to the extent that the red's magnificent pelage has.

Gray foxes put their long, nonretractable claws to good use and can climb a tree with all the lightning swiftness of a house cat or bobcat. The gray fox preys more heavily on game-bird species than the red fox does, being especially hard on ruffed grouse at times. Though both foxes prefer to hunt "edge" areas, where they can stick to cover for protection but patrol clearings,

Though not as wary as the red fox or coyote, the catlike gray fox can climb trees almost as readily as the bobcat. (Photo by Leonard Lee Rue III)

roads, power-line rights-of-way and other open spots for prey, the gray is a more nocturnal animal that seeks out heavier cover. While the red fox preys mainly on quail and pheasant (when it can get them) in farmlands and cultivated fields, the gray fox takes more ruffed grouse, which is a forest-dwelling woodland bird. Red foxes seldom den up except in the most severe weather or when hotly pursued, but grays like to spend much of their time in a den. This is partly because of the gray's more secretive ways and partly owing to the fact that, in extreme weather, its coat is simply not as efficient as its red cousin's.

The gray fox has a territory similar in size to that of the red fox and hunts it in much the same fashion. Both kill scores of mice, their primary prey, hunting by ear. After locating the tiniest rustling sound in high grass, they jump straight up in the air and pounce on the unlucky rodent, pinning it down until they can get their mouth on it. Grays cannot run as speedily or with the endurance of a red and thus aren't nearly as favored by foxhound sportsmen. Nor do they take as many rabbits as the red, though they undoubtedly take more game birds.

Grays are not as alert or intelligent as reds. They will come to a call more readily and seem to have a shorter memory about being called; thus a call stand does not need to be rested as long when you are after grays, compared to reds or coyotes. Grays do make a fine little trophy, though, either turned into a small rug (with or without an open-mouth head mount) or mounted life-size.

HUNTING THE FOXES

Hunting with Foxhounds

Hunting with foxhounds is a long-standing and old-time branch of fox sport. Actually, it is neither a shooting nor a hunting sport, since the enjoyment comes from sitting out all night with some friends and listening to a mixed pack of specially bred foxhounds pursue old Reynard all around the countryside.

In fact, foxhound sportsmen don't get along with other types of fox hunters, since they don't want to kill the fox but

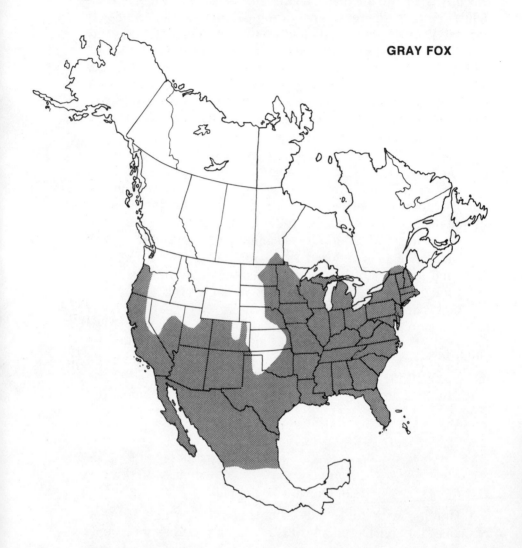

GRAY FOX

merely to enjoy the sound of the chase as their hounds rout them around the country. Reds, since they don't readily go to den and can provide a good race for six, eight or ten hours, are the preferred quarry. Grays can't run as fast and tend to go to ground, so in those areas where grays are prevalent many fox-hounders carry along a small terrier who can get into any hole the fox can. The little dog then worries the fox out into the open so the race can continue. Though the hard-running dogs may occasionally catch up with a healthy gray fox, they cannot ever run a healthy red to ground.

Hunting Opportunistically

Hunting opportunistically for foxes is similar to going after coyotes in the same fashion, except that the hunting routes are shorter and the quarry, in the case of red foxes in snow country, can be spotted somewhat more readily by the sharp-eyed winter hunter using a fresh tracking snow. Reds will lie right out in the open, tucking that long plume of a tail around them to keep their feet and underparts warm, and can sometimes be spotted on open hillsides, basking in the pale winter sun. They will even stay out in the open until completely drifted over by snow (which is a surprisingly warm insulator), but the gray fox never will. The latter always seeks the safety of a warm, well-drained den hole or hollow in the base of a big tree.

If the hunter doesn't have the benefit of a tracking snow, he will almost certainly need a good predator call (electronic, mouth or both) or some good dogs to help locate and rout out the foxes. Otherwise his foxes are strictly bonus trophies that come on a catch-as-catch-can basis while hunting other game, with the best times being early and late in the day on cold, still, overcast winter days.

The most productive time to hunt foxes, with or without a predator call, is late in the summer or early in the fall, when many of the young, naïve fox kits are almost full grown and considerably easier to bring to call or locate while tramping about the country. There are no stupid three-year-old foxes!

Calling for Foxes

Though foxes are not quite as crafty as coyotes, they test

Electronic game callers can be used for off-season wildlife photography (and to practice your calling techniques) as these two sportsmen are doing. (Photo courtesy of Johnny Stewart)

the mettle of any hunter's patience and skill—especially the red. When calling them, be sure to work good country known to have foxes around. Approach your intended calling station carefully, as if you expected to find an animal sitting right there on the spot when you arrive (which has happened to me, incidentally!). Don't make any noise slamming car doors, talking, scraping through thick brush or letting man-made objects clink together. The fox may be within thirty feet of you as you set up to call. Always pretend that he is.

Set up your calling stand so that you will be comfortable and will not continually have to shift around and make a lot of noise. *Get situated and stay put.* Pick some brushy cover, a large rock or another object to break up your outline. If calling during dawn or dusk, be sure to use camouflage netting draped around yourself and your seat for further disguise. Your hands and face are the worst giveaways, and head nets, gloves or liberal applications of camouflage cream (available at most large sporting-goods stores and archery shops) are vital.

Check your state laws thoroughly about calling at night. Some allow you to call with a light, others ban the use of a light and still others forbid night hunting entirely, restricting you to daytime hours. Other things being equal, nighttime calling is at least three times as productive as working during the first and last hour of daylight and ten times as productive as working during the midday hours.

If you can call at night, pick a still, dark-of-the-moon night with little or no wind to carry your scent and betray you. Wear dark, quiet clothing. To keep from alarming your prey any more than necessary, approach your intended calling position thus:

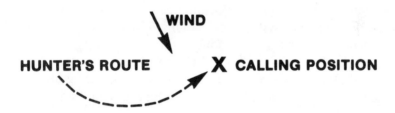

It is obvious that approaching from "above," or upwind of, the intended calling position will scatter your scent through the very area that you intend to call and ruin your hunting both upwind and downwind of your position. Even so, most of your game will try to circle around downwind of the call they hear and work up into the wind toward the noise. This is where application of some skunk scent or other scent disguiser both on your person and around your calling spot can be of great value.

Start off by playing your cassette caller (or blowing your mouth call) softly so as to coax in any nearby game without alarming it. To outfox foxes, nothing quite beats the different cottontail rabbit calls, especially the high-pitched distress squeal. In the West, the jackrabbit call can be used to vary things a bit.

Check your state laws as to restrictions on electronic calls, if any. If you can use them, they are an effective asset, but they shouldn't keep you from learning to use a simple mouth call too. A mouth call can be varied more than any tape or record to respond individually and "talk" a particular animal in. And nothing quite beats the satisfaction of fooling a highly intelligent predator with your own mouth calling. Some good callers can even do it by "kissing" the back of their hand with their mouths to imitate a rabbit's dying squeak with no mechanical means whatsoever! This gets tiring very quickly, however.

Guns for Foxes

When walking foxes up and trying to catch reds napping on snowy hillsides, a scope-sighted rifle is necessary. The .22 rimfires aren't adequate, but the .222 is fine out to 200 yards and the 22/250 and .24- and .25-caliber mediums extend this for another 75 to 150 yards.

When calling foxes in close, almost any weapon within reason will do, including quick-thinking archers with their bows. Some like to use heavy-duty handguns where the law allows. The range is often short enough, and a .357 magnum or .44-caliber revolver will certainly kill them cleanly. Other hunters prefer shotguns, relying on full or modified 12-gauge guns, shooting magnum-loaded number 2s or 4s. Buckshot isn't necessary at all.

This patented mouth call is unique in that the small, squeezable rubber bulb in the mouthpiece can be depressed by the caller's teeth to vary the tone as well as the volume. This makes the call much more flexible. (Photo courtesy of Johnny Stewart)

This hunter lured his red fox in during a winter calling session and took him at close range with a shotgun loaded with number 2 shot. (Photo by Leonard Lee Rue III)

159

All these guns have advantages and disadvantages, but as a matter of personal preference, I like to take my foxes with centerfire rifles—this in spite of the fact that a heavy-duty handgun would be as efficient close in and a shotgun even more efficient. Guess I'm just a rifleman at heart. It seems more appropriate for these little trophies.

A Final Tip

Scent is the nighttime caller's biggest bugaboo. Do some experimenting. Check with various sportsmen to see what scents they use. Some come up with weird but effective homemade concoctions that are mixes of several commercial scent maskers, while others start from scratch and come up with strange and wondrous aromas quite unlike anything in nature. Arguments over the efficacy of these various olfactory wonders add interest and spice to the sport. Check different sporting-goods stores and mail-order houses. Some of the apple-based deer-hunting scent maskers have been very effective at times. Keep looking and keep experimenting. That's what it takes to put a well-furred fox on your family room wall.

Outlook for Foxes and Fox Hunting

Foxes are hardy animals that seem to have profited from the coming of the white man with his land clearing and his eradication of many larger competitive predators. The gray fox, originally more a southern animal, has extended its range northward, while the red, more a northerly animal, has moved south in numbers. Though foxes take some toll of game animals, it has never been proven that they have a significant sustained impact on any prey species, and aside from the red's depredations on the farmer's poults, there is no great amount of conflict with man.

With the price of fur skyrocketing in recent years, it may be that additional restrictions on the fur trapper will be necessary. But especially since more and more states are placing season and bag limits on foxes and managing them as a game animal rather than as a furbearer or as vermin, foxes would appear to have a good future as a sporting game animal and attractive trophy.

160

10

Bagging Your Bobcat

Johnny Stewart, the veteran Texas game-call maker, delights in telling the story of his first calling adventure. He and a friend, with all the confidence of the uninitiated, set out many years ago with a homemade record-player-type caller and an equally homemade recording of a rabbit in distress. They set up to call in an area neither of them knew well, a bit east of Laredo, in the middle of a scorching hot day. Their bag: two bobcats called up to practically arm's length, both in the heat of the day.

Stewart tells this true anecdote to emphasize one central point: All wild animals are unpredictable and none more so than the bobcat. To that I add fervent agreement! One thing to remember when reading about the various species in this or any other hunting book is that wild animals, not being able to read such books, do not always know what they are "supposed" to do and when and how they are "supposed" to do it!

Wild animals are primarily (some say solely, but I do not agree) creatures of instinct. Thus we can predict what they will usually do under a given set of circumstances. But all wild things are wondrously unpredictable, and none more so than the wild cats. The thing aspiring hunters must do is learn about their quarry—its normal patterns of behavior, food preferences and methods of hunting for food—and then, if all else fails, be prepared to try the unorthodox. By all the laws of reason and good sense, Stewart and his buddy should never have been able to blunder into a strange area during the height of the daylight hours and call up not one but two animals that hunters call and kill less frequently than any other. But they did just that.

ABOUT THE BOBCAT

The bobcat (so named for its short "bobbed" tail) is an intelligent, highly adaptable predator. Due to their rangy, leggy appearance and the fact that they are also wildcats, bobcats are almost always considerably overestimated in size by hunters who have not been around them very much. Actually, the bobcat averages only about 18 to 25 pounds in weight, or about twice as heavy as a fox but usually a bit smaller than a coyote and considerably smaller than a lynx. It stands about 22 inches at the shoulder; northern bobcats are usually larger than southern cats, while western cats are usually larger (and grayer) than eastern animals. Bobcats vary widely in color with dense-forest-dwelling animals of the northern regions being darker and grayer than the paler more buff-toned animals of the southwestern deserts. Wherever it is found, the bobcat is one of our most beautifully colored and marked animals. A bobcat trophy, either made into a rug or mounted lifesize, is an attractive addition to any trophy room.

The bobcat is a classic cat and, as such, lives and hunts in a fashion totally different from that of the foxes, coyotes and other wild canids. Whereas the latter exhibit varying degrees of sociability and cooperation when hunting and rearing young, the bobcat is a solitary wanderer that has never developed any pronounced social order beyond the most rudimentary one of the mother's attachment for her young.

The bobcat depends upon stealth and is even more nocturnal than the fox and coyote. The bobcat's primary prey species is the rabbit or the hare, as is that of the more northerly dwelling lynx, but the bobcat has proven itself much more adaptable and readily takes mice, rats, squirrels, chipmunks and porcupines and, at times, game birds and livestock or poultry as well.

Bobcats, more often than the canids, lie in wait and ambush their prey, as does the much larger cougar. Though bobcats are usually much more thinly populated than coyotes, probably each requiring a home range some two to three times larger than the latter, the bobcat will often not cover as much ground during any given night of hunting.

162

The bobcat is an elusive prize demanding skill and persistence from the small game hunter, but a trophy well worth the effort!

This is partly owing to the bobcat's penchant for ambushes, but it also relates to the fact that, even though it's a leggy animal, the bobcat doesn't have the wide-ranging endurance of the dog-like predators. Cats and canines kill entirely differently. The canines are relatively slow animals with enormous endurance that can lope along for hours on end at cruising speed. The cats have enormous initial speed and for the first 200 to 400 yards, depending upon the particular species and the terrain, are among our fastest animals. Everyone is well acquainted with the cheetah's legendary speed, but some don't realize how briefly he

163

can maintain it. Bobcats, like others of their tribe, simply don't have the lungs to enable them to run for hours. Though bobcats move with blurring speed when making a quick dash or a lightning-swift pounce on unsuspecting prey, they don't like to run. When forced to do so they will bound along in leaps of 8 to 10 feet, but they can only attain a top speed of about 15 miles per hour.

Bobcats are quick, efficient killers, pouncing on their prey and impaling them with stilettolike teeth designed for stabbing deep and holding on. Their claws enable them to cling to their quarry and, if it is a large animal, actually ride it down and wrench its neck. The doglike predators, in contrast, are generally messier, less efficient killers, with long muzzles and slashing teeth designed for raking slashes that disable larger prey and kill it more slowly. Of course, a coyote or fox will kill rodents or cottontail rabbits with ease and dispatch owing to the small size and weakness of these prey species.

Though no danger to man as some of the more purple stories in our folklore might have it, bobcats are tremendously powerful animals. Cats weighing less than 20 pounds have been known to kill full-grown deer, though this usually occurred when the deer were handicapped by deep snow or winter weakness. When pursued by dogs, they can usually kill any single dog—unless it is an extremely large and experienced hound. This in spite of the fact that the dog is usually three to four times as large as the cat!

Bobcats have probably never been very plentiful, and there may now be more of them around in many areas than ever before. The reason for their low density has never been fully determined. It certainly isn't because of their lack of adaptability. They are one of the few animals equally at home on the timbered slopes of the Rocky Mountain West, in the arid wastes of the southwestern deserts, in the piney-wood swamps of the Deep South or in the hardwood forests of the East. And they have learned to take a wide variety of prey. All told, bobcats have profited from the coming of the white man, because though they often do prefer to live in more heavily wooded areas than the coyote and red fox, they like to hunt the "edge" areas where man and his grain fields attract the rodents they seek as prey.

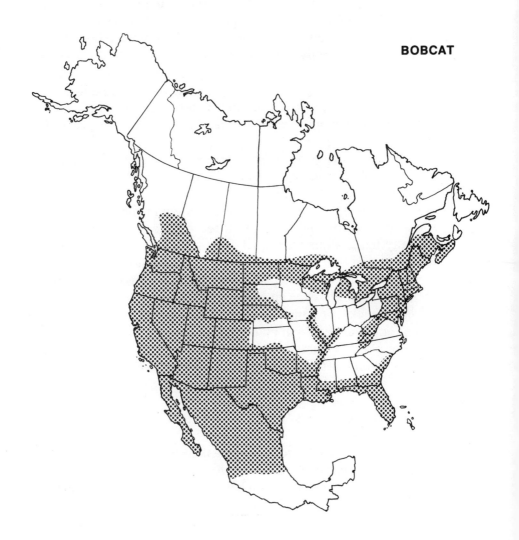

BOBCAT

Since the coming of the white man, bobcats have extended their geographical range as well as their numbers (though they seem to be being inexorably squeezed out of some Mississippi Valley areas) because of logging and land-clearing activities that have converted many areas of sterile climax forest into cutover areas harboring more prey. Bobcats prefer half-open country with lots of openings and brushy patches. The broken terrain gives them more prey to hunt and better ambush spots, and yet the forest remnants give them the thick cover they prefer for their own refuge.

While how the bobcat compares with the gray and red foxes and the coyote in intelligence can be argued endlessly, there is no doubt that this cat is an extremely intelligent animal. It is more nocturnal, more stealthy, more deliberate and generally more of a heavy-cover animal than the three canine predators (though the gray fox is almost an equal in its preference for heavy cover to den in and flee to when pressed). Incidentally, when hunting any species opportunistically, don't hesitate to (legally) explore the attics, cellars or even main living areas of old, abandoned cabins, shacks or ranch houses. Bobcats know a good thing when they see it and will many times set up housekeeping in one of these old structures, rather than in a natural den, if the building is seldom disturbed or visited by people.

ARE BOBCATS "GOOD" OR "BAD" ANIMALS?

This unfortunate question is asked about various animals, but probably more often about the bobcat than any other. Of course, the simple and somewhat incomplete answer is that one man's flower is another's weed. As we have already discovered, bobcats are not "ferocious" or a direct menace to man. The only records I have of people being attacked are a very few instances where a cornered cat that has been trapped and held by a leg-hold trap has attempted to attack a person coming too near.

Bobcats do occasionally raid the farmer's livestock or poultry, but this is almost always the work of a single animal that has learned about this easy meal ticket rather than a widespread practice among all cats. Bobcats do take game birds and are especially fond of wild turkey where the latter abound. But it has never been proven that wildcats have had any significant negative impact on any of their prey species. They merely seem to take a harvestable surplus, except in a few localized instances.

Practically all states have stopped the outmoded practice of paying a bounty on these animals, and most regulate the animal as a game species, complete with season and bag limits. Some states have completely closed the season on them, both for hunting and trapping, in order to protect them more fully as more people have come to appreciate them.

Though bobcat fur is very pretty, it is relatively short and stiff as cat fur goes and was never in demand in the luxury fur market until recent years. With many species of cat now declared off limits for the commercial fur trade, however, bobcats have borne the brunt of this demand and fur prices for their pelts have skyrocketed in recent years. The result has been tighter trapping restrictions in most areas and complete closing of the trapping season on the cats in many states. This better ensures an adequate supply of the bobcat as a game animal in those areas with huntable populations.

On balance, the bobcat is an attractive, interesting animal that, like the bear and the eagle, adds much to our woods just by *being* there.

HUNTING THE BOBCAT

Candidly speaking, bobcats are by far the toughest to take of all small game. They have never been very numerous and they are extremely wary and nocturnal. I spend many weeks of the year tramping woods all over the continent, and I have only twice seen bobcats out during the day when I did not have the aid of hounds or predator-calling devices. You do occasionally see them streaking across country roads at night when they are surprised by your headlights, but chances are you could live in good bobcat country all your life and never just stumble upon one by yourself during the day. This, for all practical purposes,

Most bobcats are taken by calling. Rarely are they the result of a chance encounter in the woods such as this one, where a cat that has just killed a cottontail is about to be surprised by a hunter looking for deer.

does away with any significant chance to take them while hunting opportunistically.

Hunting Bobcats with Hounds

Using hounds really isn't a good way for the average man to hunt bobcats on his own. For one thing, a pack of four or five cat dogs takes some room and expense to keep up—far more than the occasional hunter can justify. For another, good, well-trained cat dogs can hardly be bought anywhere. It is relatively easy to get dogs with good aptitude for this hunting, but the sport is specialized enough that individuals must usually develop their own dogs. To do that you should have a thorough knowledge of dogs and bobcats, live in good cat country and be able to work them occasionally with other already-developed dogs.

Hunting bobcats with hounds is somewhat different from using hounds for foxes. The latter sport is entirely nocturnal (except when some of the longer races extend over into the early morning daylight hours) and is strictly a dog man's sport, with killing looked down upon. Coursing bobcats with hounds is very different. The hounds are turned loose on a fresh track during the morning, and they usually bay up or tree the cat pretty quickly after they locate him. What fun there is to this sport is the excitement of wondering if they will actually locate the cat and the entertainment of listening to the dog music during the race.

Once the bobcat is treed, most of the sport is over, and though a cat occasionally bails out of a tree and the race is on again, it usually is a pretty set-piece affair of shooting the treed cat with most any small-caliber rifle or revolver at rather close range. If one must have a bobcat trophy, probably the surest bet is to hire a hunting guide who keeps a specially trained pack of dogs and who specializes in this type of hunting. Good, reputable operators of this sort can be located in ads in the back of the major national sporting magazines. This technique is available mostly in the East in Maine and in the West in Colorado and several other Rocky Mountain states.

Hunting Bobcats with a Predator Call

Bobcats are considerably more alert and exhibit more curiosity than domestic house cats. In common with almost all the cats, they are primarily sight hunters, though they have superb hearing. Their sense of smell, while far keener than a man's, is of less importance to them than to the fox or coyote. If your state law allows, you will find night calling for bobcats far more effective than daylight work. If you must restrict yourself to daylight calling, the first hour after dawn is when you will get the majority of your action.

Johnny Stewart and others who have had far more cat-calling experience that I have had are convinced that bobcats are

Actually, bobcats aren't as difficult to call in as are coyotes. They just seem to be more difficult because there are far fewer cats and thus they are taken less often. These two hunters each took a prized cat during a daytime hunt, proving that these night-loving cats can also be taken during the day.

easier to call in than coyotes (though not as easy as foxes). They *seem* to be more difficult (and results are much lower) simply because there are far fewer cats around. Also, they are more nocturnal, and this hurts callers restricted solely to daylight hunting. Finally, bobcats are famous among callers as being, if not more wary and intelligent than coyotes, considerably more *deliberate*. Whereas in good coyote country fifteen to twenty minutes (sometimes even less) is ample time to allow per calling stand, when you are after cats thirty minutes to an hour is none too long. Cats will often take much longer to come in—coming a

Bobcats are deliberate animals, usually taking longer to come to a call than coyotes or foxes. Stay on your stand for thirty to forty-five minutes and longer in good cat country before moving on. (Photo courtesy of WYOMING FISH & GAME DEPARTMENT*)*

hundred yards or so, pausing and sitting and watching and listening and then coming another hundred yards or so.

When calling for bobcats, allow extra time and *don't move.* Stories abound about callers who worked an area for fifteen or twenty minutes and then picked up to leave, only to discover fresh cat tracks where there had been none before. These tracks show that the cat had approached within fifty or a hundred yards of the caller and merely sat there, debating whether to come on in, until the caller had aborted the calling session and frightened it away. If there is good cat sign around, even forty-five minutes to an hour is not too long to devote to working a good area. This of course means that the cat callers cannot cover nearly as much country as their fox- and coyote-calling counterparts. This, too, serves to lower the already-slim success ratio.

Since bobcats are not primarily scent hunters, they'll come

Camouflage of the highest order is necessary when hunting bobcats during the day. Note how camo netting hides this hunter so well that you can hardly see him (we left his hands and face white and didn't put him back farther into the brush so you could see him). To complete the effect, use camo-net head nets and gloves or smear these highly visible areas with camouflage grease sold at most archery shops.

to a call from upwind about as readily as to a call from downwind. This is in sharp contrast to the canids, which will circle in and come from downwind nine times out of ten. However, the keen-sighted cat will use every bit of cover to hide behind. And that mottled coat is marvelously effective camouflage. Stay alert! When a cat comes in during the daytime, it will invariably be in your lap before you know it. Try to position the speaker of your electronic call (or yourself if you're mouth calling) so that the cat has to cross some sort of clearing or open area to get to the call. When working at night, use an amber or, better yet, reddish-tinted light pointed upward at a 45-degree angle to spot the cat's telltale eyeshine.

The bobcat caller should watch all directions much more

alertly than the fox and coyote hunter. That cat can come in at any time from any direction. Though a coon will come to a squeaking-woodpecker or other bird-in-distress call, the foxes and coyotes tend to limit themselves more to rabbit-in-distress calls—both cottontails and jackrabbits in the case of the coyote. The bobcat, being intensely curious, seems to come to the squeaking-bird call a bit more readily than the canines. When I'm about ready to give up on a calling station after fruitlessly bombarding the countryside with rabbit screams for forty-five minutes or so, I usually try the birdcall, and I've even had a cat come to a squealing-javelina call!

As with any other kind of hunting, if the textbook approach isn't working, try the unorthodox. What have you got to lose? Cat hunting is never very productive, and it's for the patient and determined hunters who have their hearts set on a bobcat trophy. That doesn't mean you won't go out and, like John Stewart, get one up in broad daylight on your first foray. But don't count on it!

EATING BOBCAT

Though I have never eaten bobcat, several people have told me that the rather whitish, close-grained meat is quite good. This is disputed by others. However, this would appear to be in line with the fact that the early settlers considered cougar a delicacy, especially in those areas where pork wasn't available. Worldwide, the Chinese and some others have relished the wild cats as meat over the centuries, partly for medicinal properties real or imagined by their culture. In any event, the bobcat is hunted as a sport and trophy animal and has never been considered primarily a meat animal.

GUNS FOR BOBCAT

A bobcat is a tough animal, but it isn't particularly large or thick-skinned. Of course, as with any other animal, a lot depends upon whether the animal is alarmed, pumping adrenaline and therefore much more difficult to kill.

I do not recommend using .22 rimfires for cat hunting, however, even when shooting them out of a tree when bayed up by hounds. Any of the .22 centerfires will do fine, as will the .24- and .25-caliber deer rifles. Large-caliber handguns from the .357 magnum on up will do fine, assuming the handgunner does his part on bullet placement. Many cats have been killed with a .38 Special over the years, though I would not consider it to be ideal under some conditions. Actually, since cats are few and far enough between, I would recommend a rifle when calling them, even though they are usually called within handgun range. Unless you are an accomplished handgunner (most of us aren't), and unless you feel you simply must take your cat trophy with a short gun, why take a chance on missing that precious and relatively rare trophy with the short-barreled gun? Killing your first bobcat in the flesh is not like putting a round in the black at the fifty-foot target range!

Bobcats, since they are definitely a trophy animal with most of us, are better taken during the cooler periods of the year when that fine little pelt is in good condition. Good luck on your cat hunting. When you finally do get one, chances are you will have earned him ten times over, but the trophy will be all the more precious for that fact!

PART III

Precision Small Game Hunting and Pest Shooting

11

Connecting on Chucks

There has been a mild sort of revolution in one end of small game hunting within the last generation or so. Though the various rabbits, tree squirrels and upland birds have been avidly pursued since colonial times, the interest in woodchuck hunting (and rock chucking in the West) is relatively recent. Up until about thirty years ago, chucks were shot occasionally as pests by farmers and livestock owners. When grazing in top form in the summer pastures, a fat woodchuck can consume approximately its own weight in greens each day! Also, the well-known "chuckholes" can be dangerous to both people and livestock in densely used areas.

Then, in the 1930s and (after an interruption for World War II) the late 1940s, a number of experimental-minded gun nuts developed certain high-velocity .22-centerfire cartridges that were "wildcats" (not offered in off-the-shelf factory loadings) primarily for long-range precision shooting at the eastern woodchuck. Much of this early developmental work was done by men in my own state of Pennsylvania, which has since colonial days shown a penchant for fine rifled firearms and precision shooting.

Though the factories did offer some limited cartridges and rifles for this type of shooting, much of it was still confined to special-interest groups that had the time and money to develop their own rifles and cartridges. Starting in the 1950s, the woodchuck began to expand greatly both in range and in numbers in the East, owing to the trend toward "permanent pasturage" among many landowners. There are far more chucks in many

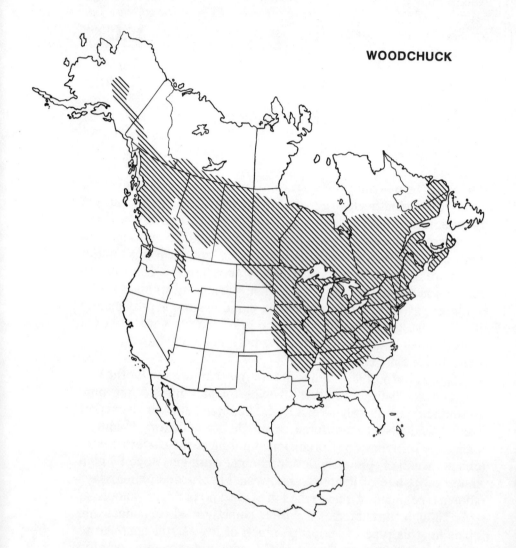

WOODCHUCK

areas of their range right now than has ever been the case before. About this time, due to the inroads made upon their sales by certain small but nevertheless "factory" gun makers who sprang up, the "majors" in the gun trade finally caught on and either started offering standardized weapons for many cartridges that had heretofore been strictly "wildcats" or, in other cases, developed their own outstanding new .22 and .24 centerfires that were ideal for chucking. The period since the early 1960s has seen a literal explosion of interest in chuck shooting, to the extent that many states are now wisely regulating them as game animals rather than leaving them in the completely unprotected "varmint" category.

There are a number of chucks in North America, but the Olympic and Vancouver marmots of the Far West are too localized to be of any significant interest, and the large, hoary marmot ("whistler") ranges too far north of the U.S. border. When we speak of chuck hunting, we really refer to the woodchuck in the East and the yellow-bellied marmot, or rock chuck, in the West.

ABOUT THE EASTERN WOODCHUCK

The woodchuck (which has a variety of names, from groundhog, marmot, chuck, clover clipper and whistle pig on through the limited southern term of monax) is closely related to a group of animals we've already talked about—the squirrels. This chunky, dark-brown animal has a short, bushy tail and legs so short they are often hard to see when it is walking. The animal inhabits the old world as well as the new, and though the basic body color is brown, the long gray ends of the guard hairs often give the back a grizzled-gray appearance. This fat, tubular-shaped animal is about the size of a large house cat. It generally weighs between 8 and 10 pounds when prime during the summer season, and the largest I have ever personally verified weighed a little shy of 13 pounds. It runs 24 to 26 inches in length, and because of those very short legs it is among the slowest of all

179

Here he is, the eastern woodchuck or ground hog. Known by a variety of aliases from "whistle pig" to "clover clipper," he's a sporty long-distance rifleman's target whatever you call him!

mammals of its size. A fat chuck can only manage about 6 to 8 miles per hour and, along with the raccoon, is one of the few animals that an athletic man can actually run down on open ground.

Woodchucks know they are extremely slow and vulnerable when out of their burrows, so this makes them watchful and, where hunted, doubly wary. Dogs can easily catch them and thus are a big enemy. Though most mammals are more or less nocturnal, if there ever was a sun-loving creature of the daytime it's the chunky chuck. Near their feeding grounds these burrowing animals create tunnels and dens that they live in and flee to when in danger. They don't like to travel for the simple reason that they don't move well and don't like to be exposed, so a chuck will seldom venture more than fifteen hundred feet from its burrow, preferring to stay within two hundred feet. When moving farther afield, chucks will sometimes have escape holes available to flee to when pressed.

Woodchucks love most things green, but alfalfa and clover top the list. They also readily consume soybeans, corn, beans, peas, lettuce and all manner of other things that the farmer doesn't want to share. Chucks are colonial animals, living together in groups rather than singly. When you figure that during the height of their feeding season when they are storing up fat for the summer hibernation, a hundred chucks (not a lot in good chuck country) can easily "harvest" half a ton of these desirable greens and vegetables each day, it's no wonder that most farmers are cooperative when you offer to help control their chuck population!

ABOUT THE ROCK CHUCK

Though similar in appearance to the eastern woodchuck, the rock chuck or yellow-bellied marmot is a somewhat larger animal. These western chucks will, in the case of a summer-prime adult, average about 2 inches longer (up to 28 inches) and weigh 2 or 3 pounds more. Since the American West is itself a huge, high plateau with the lowlands often ranging from 3,500 to over 5,000 feet, these are high-country animals. South of the Canadian border they will be found living as high as 10,000 feet up, though farther to the north they and their northern cousins, the hoary marmots, will not range so high.

Both the rock chuck and the hoary marmot show a more pronounced tendency to utter a whistling or keening alarm sound. This is why both animals are so often referred to as "whistlers" or "whistle pigs" by the natives. This high-pitched, at times almost eerie sound is truly a sound of the mountains and one that I love to hear, along with the bugling of elk, the howling of coyotes and the honking of Canada geese.

Rock chucks are very similar to woodchucks, but the difference in their habitat does cause some differences in their habits. Since the rock chuck is subject to more predators that try to dig them out (ranging from badgers to grizzly bears), they tend to be found among rock slides. These rocky fortresses give them a bit more protection either as dens or just as places to seek tempo-

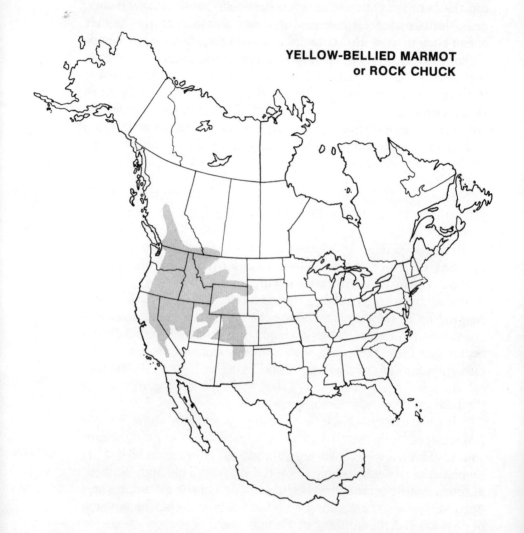

YELLOW-BELLIED MARMOT or ROCK CHUCK

rary refuge. Thus they are forced to travel more than eastern chucks in order to descend to the greener valleys and feed.

Also, because of their larger size and the higher, colder world they live in, they must eat more than the eastern woodchuck. Though rock chucks will readily take alfalfa and cultivated vegetables, the major part of their food is limited to the various grasses and forbs of the high alpine meadows because of their normal distance from most farms. Like the woodchuck, the rock chuck depends primarily on its eyesight for survival, sitting up regularly on a large rock or other slight prominence to search for danger. They also hear extremely well, so don't make undue noises when stalking them.

Though the yellow-bellied marmot is not nearly as hotly pursued by man and domestic dogs, it does have many wild predators to contend with that are not a factor with the eastern chuck. Golden eagles probably take more rock chucks than any other predators, but lynxes, bobcats, foxes, grizzlies and others also share a taste for chuck meat.

If the fat and membranes are removed, woodchucks and rock chucks are very good eating—especially the younger animals. It's no accident that Indians from the East Coast to the Rockies to the Cassiars and Alaska Range have always prized chucks highly as food.

HUNTING THE EASTERN WOODCHUCK

Though woodchucks have expanded their range and population considerably in the last twenty years, there has been at least a comparable growth in shooting interest for these animals. Thus, most progressive states have seen fit to afford them varying degrees of protection, especially during their breeding season. This is all to the good.

Woodchuck hunting is strictly a rifleman's sport, with the scatter-guns having no application. The standard .22s, up to and including the high-velocity loadings of the .22 long rifle, simply are not flat enough shooting or powerful enough for a proper woodchuck gun. Though many thousands of chucks have been

The yellow-bellied marmot or rock chuck, the larger-sized western edition of the eastern woodchuck, is usually taken at longer ranges in windier country—requiring more powerful rifles. (Photo by Leonard Lee Rue III)

killed by these guns in the hands of barefoot farm boys over the years, all too many of the animals were wounded and escaped to die in agony in their dens. This is not acceptable, for the true sportsman is concerned with making as clean a kill on these animals as on the larger and more glamorous big game species.

The twice-as-powerful .22 WRF and 5mm Remington magnum rounds can be used on chucks out to a bit better than a hundred yards, but real chuck guns start with the .22 hornet and .218 bee class of centerfire .22s and work upward in power. These guns are flat-shooting enough for good medium- to long-range sport and powerful enough to kill cleanly at those ranges.

Through the years the classic method of chuck hunting was to cruise the back roads in vehicles, glassing the rolling grassy hillsides and meadows for either the "picket pin" look of a chuck sitting up or the telltale mound of fresh earth signaling an active chuck den (and thus nearby game). The shooting was often accomplished over the hood of the vehicle itself. This is now a bit out of date, since states have ever more stringent laws about shooting from roads (even secondaries and farm lanes) or shooting from vehicles even in fields. Check your state laws carefully on this point! These laws are changeable and generally well enforced.

However, you can still cruise the back roads looking for game and then depart on a foot stalk after locating it. Always check with the farmer or landowner for permission. Sometimes it's a good idea to engage the farmer in a bit of general, casual conversation about the area and his farm, something he's usually ready to talk about unless busy at the moment, before actually broaching the subject of chuck hunting. (See Appendix I for more tips on this sensitive and important subject of securing landowner permission to hunt small game.)

Some chuck hunters develop a good enough network so that their farmer friends call *them* each year when it's chuck time and suggest they come up, even giving them tips as to where the most chuck activity seems to be that year. This is not unusual when you have proven yourself to a farmer after a year or two of chucking on his land. Respecting his fences and livestock and not bringing too many other hunters or hunting his land too often are the basics of proving oneself in such instances.

185

Lots of den holes (like the one immediately to the right of the rifle) with their telltale mounds of fresh earth (under the sunglasses) mean lots of good chuck hunting and hazards for the farmer's implements and live-stock. This chuck was nailed just after leaving the den.

You should try to develop a number of farms in several areas so that you don't have to shoot any single farm too often or too heavily. Though both eastern and western chucks are relatively prolific animals (the eastern animals normally bear litters of four young and the western animals, having more natural enemies and living in harsher environments, bear litters of six to eight),

186

it's the wise sportsman who "farms" game and does not over-shoot it. In fact, even though most farmers want their chucks controlled, the more progressive ones among them usually don't want the animal totally eradicated.

The chuck hunter needs a good pair of binoculars—and I mean just that: a *good* pair. You are trying to locate rather small targets that are neutral colored and at long range. This calls for glasses with good resolving ability of 8x to 10x. Simply getting "high-power" cheapies doesn't do it; they may offer more out-right optical power, but they don't offer the necessary optical precision. Swift, Bushnell and Tasco make good-quality afford-able glasses for the budget-minded chuck hunter.

A good spotting scope with small tripod is not absolutely necessary but it can (especially for the western rock-chucker) make things both more productive and more fun. Chuck hunters will do well to have some sort of bipod or other elevatable rifle rest, since they will sometimes be shooting from high-grass fields where they cannot assume the ultra-steady prone position and there are no natural objects (rocks, trees, etc.) around to rest on. There are several makes of relatively inexpensive rifle bipods (with padded rests to lay the rifle fore-end or barrel on) available for about $10 in larger sporting-goods stores. Also, homemade rests can be fashioned from old camera tripods or ski poles. Just be sure you never rest the rifle, either its wood fore-end or the barrel itself, against a *hard* object to shoot. This usually throws off the point of impact.

Chucking is precision shooting. However, the rifleman shooting one of the lower-powered .22 centerfires (say, from the .222 downward) can usually take most shots from within 200 yards. Some real devotees of the game, shooting the higher-powered .22s, .24s and 6mms, will *back off* in order to take those more sporting 250- to 350-yard shots. One good thing about shooting these powerful guns at this small target at such long ranges is the fact that each shot is always either a clean miss or a good kill.

Actually, in the East where noise is sometimes a problem, it's usually a good idea to carry along one of the milder-voiced .22s and also a heavier-duty .22 or .24. This way you have two

Many dedicated chuck shooters turn to heavy-barreled, ultra-accurate "varmint model" rifles for the demanding shooting required to take chucks and crows at very long ranges. This special "varmint model" of the basic Model 70 Winchester is an example of one of the best. (Photo courtesy of WINCHESTER-WESTERN*)*

guns with you that can handle both the nearer shots and the longer targets sportingly and yet, in more densely populated areas, with a minimum of noise when desirable. The chuck hunter should be extremely safety conscious, never firing unless absolutely sure there is a backstop to catch the bullet and keep it from ricocheting. One of the shooting ironies of this sport is that the louder calibers are actually at least as safe as the lower-powered calibers, due to the fact that their higher-velocity bullets almost always explode properly on impact without ricocheting, no matter how long the range. But many nonshooters associate noise with danger. A good combination for an eastern hunter would be a .222 and a .243. The former would give good sport to 225 yards and not much recoil or noise, while the latter would, with the proper 80-grain bullets, give good sport out beyond 300 yards and excellent training for using the same rifle (with more heavily constructed 100-grain bullets) for deer and other game in the fall.

Rifle scopes are fully as important to this demanding sport as the rifles themselves. A 4x hunting scope just doesn't get the nod. A 6x scope is minimum, but a still better idea is one of the better-quality 2x to 7x or 3x to 9x vari-power scopes that can be used on more than one rifle. This single scope can be used for big game, when set at the lower powers, and then does quite well for chuck hunting when set from 7x to 9x. For the really serious long-range chuck hunter, there are special target scopes of far higher power that offer extremely good resolving power at high magnifications.

When woodchuck hunting, camouflage clothing is a good idea, as is a knowledge of the area you are hunting. Chucks that aren't chased by dogs or hunted too frequently will often let a hunter approach within 200 yards or even a bit nearer. Those that have been hassled a bit are far more wary. It's best to move only when the chuck is down on all fours eating and to remain stationary (crouched over to destroy that telltale man silhouette) when they are sitting up for their periodic visual safety check. It's best to shoot them in this upright position, however, as they then afford a considerably larger target. Chuck hunting with a buddy is best. That means two sets of eyes to locate the game, someone to help call your shots when you miss, and someone to share all the fun with.

Chuck hunting should be approached qualitatively and not quantitatively. That's why, though perhaps it's mostly a matter of semantics, I'm not in love with the term "varmint hunting." Chucks are a fine little game animal, and in this era "varmint" shooting seems to imply a certain amount of excess that was acceptable in another time but seems a bit out of step today.

Good chuck hunters exercise restraint when, even though the season may be open on chucks, there are still a lot of rather stupid half-grown juveniles around that can be shot off too easily. Determining how many chucks to harvest from each farm, turning each stalk and shot into a planned adventure and savoring the experience makes it a great sport that helps round out the small game hunter's year when most other game is out of season. Excessive shooting is not necessary.

HUNTING THE WESTERN ROCK CHUCK

As you might anticipate, there are many similarities in the hunting of the two chucks. However, since the western chucks live in higher, windier areas, the .24- and .25-caliber centerfires with their heavier bullets, that aren't so subject to wind drift at long range, really come into their own here. Then again, noise is usually less of a factor, which removes the penalty against these more powerful calibers.

189

Though woodchucks are prolific animals that have prospered with the coming of civilization, easy-to-kill half-grown juveniles such as these two should not be overharvested. A year from now these two will have an I.Q. about three times as high!

Also, spring black bear hunting is often open in many of the good rock-chucking areas, and having the larger caliber at hand can be convenient. I believe that, in years to come, more and more eastern sportsmen will consider taking their youngsters west for a combination small game safari and black bear hunt. This way they will avoid much of the crowds and expense associated with the fall big game hunts and get to enjoy some of the most magnificent country on earth during the balmier weather of

190

spring and early summer. Contact the western fish and game departments for more information. A simple request addressed to:

(state) _____ Fish & Game Department
(state capital) _____ , (state) _____
Att: Request for hunting information

will easily secure you the information. This type of trip will guarantee your youngster some good shooting, with the glamorous off chance of seeing or perhaps taking a black bear. And for a bargain price in most cases, too!

Though you should always be safety conscious and alert to the effects of your shooting, safety is generally not quite the consideration in these less-settled rock-chuck areas that it is in the East. However, be aware of ricochet possibilities when shooting at big rock chucks sitting in rock-slide areas.

Not only is this windier country than the East, it is more open and the animal is often warier, more because of the abundance of natural predators than due to sport hunting by man. Thus, longer shots are often necessary and it may be that you have to stalk closer no matter how powerful your cartridge. If so, remember that rock chucks, like most mountain game, can often be more readily approached from behind and above than from below.

Here again, emphasizing the qualitative aspects of this shooting is a fine idea. With a bit of imagination you can pretend you are stalking and shooting a magnificent Dall or stone sheep rather than a rock chuck. Actually, the rock chuck is often as hard to stalk and much harder to hit. If you can consistently score on grizzled old slide sitters, you're going to be ready for that once-in-a-lifetime Far North sheep hunt when it comes along!

12

Cleaning Up on Crows

My candidate for the wariest, wiliest bird on this continent would be the raven. Next would come the raven's close relative, the common crow. Crows are fascinating birds, with an "infuriation quotient" (as you'll quickly learn when you begin to hunt them) hardly matched by any other creature, whether finned, furred or feathered. Crows see with a piercing vision hardly outreached by the hawks and eagles, and they *learn* from that vision. Crows learn quickly enough that people in moving cars are no danger, but let the driver stop the car and get out and things change. In some areas where they are consistently hunted, crows learn the difference between a man with a gun (a hunter) and a man with other implements in his hands (a harmless farmer). The distance at which they will allow the two to approach them without flying off is vastly different!

The common crow is about 17 inches in length, or just a tad smaller than an adult red-shouldered hawk. At a distance you can tell them from any of the several hawks they might be confused with by the fact that crows fly with a much steadier, flapping flight, seldom going more than two to three seconds without flapping their wings. Hawks glide more, even when they're flying in their version of flapping flight.

Crows are abundant almost everywhere in the East, and they are locally abundant throughout much of the West except in the most arid parts. Due to changing land-use patterns, plus the protection they have been receiving in recent years from closed seasons, crows have probably never been more abundant. Some eastern areas are experiencing crow population explosions.

Crow hunting used to be a simple and straightforward pastime. Crows were classified as varmints, and the hunting on them was open year-round with no regulations on the number that could be killed or the time of day or year they could be taken. No more. The U.S. government attempted to negotiate a treaty with the Mexican government to protect several migratory bird species that move back and forth between the two countries. The story goes that the Mexicans insisted the treaty cover the entire major bird family Corvidae, which—you guessed it— includes the crows, ravens and jays, among others. So, without its necessarily being intended, crows are now a "protected" game species throughout the entire United States, with limitations on when they may be hunted.

This development has, for numerous reasons, caused a large amount of confusion among the various state fish and game departments that must implement this federal covenant. Some, such as the one in Alaska, have flatly refused to recognize (or tried to) the federal government's right to do this. All have been confused and are "enforcing" these regulations in a wide variety of ways and with widely varying degrees of stringency. Basically, the situation is that crows can be hunted during approximately 120 days of the year, if this period does not include the breeding and fledging season. My advice is to check your state fish and game regulations on crow shooting carefully and then, if you're especially interested in this brand of sport, call one of the branch offices and ask for a personal interpretation of any points that may confuse you.

At one time of the year or another, crows inhabit each of the contiguous forty-eight states, and there are substantial year-round resident breeding populations in most of them. Though crows are migratory, like geese and many other migrants of the modern era, there are now many resident populations that do not find it necessary to move with the seasons because of the good living afforded by civilized man and his crops. Others continue to move south in the winter and north in the summer as their ancestors did before them.

There are two methods of crow hunting involving almost diametrically opposite approaches and kinds of equipment.

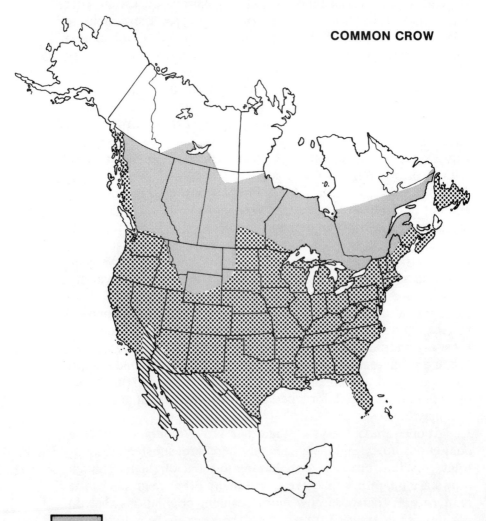

COMMON CROW

Summer Range

Winter Range

All Year

CALLING CROWS TO THE SHOTGUN

Probably somewhere between 85 and 90 percent of the crows killed by sportsmen each year are taken by shotgun. Crows tend to establish fairly consistent flyways between their feeding grounds and their roosting areas. They fly from the roosts around dawn or a bit later each morning, feed for a while and then return. In the late afternoon they follow the same pattern.

The first requirement of crow hunting is to learn these flight patterns. You can do this by cruising farm-country roads early and late and by getting to know some farmers and asking them to keep a lookout for you. Once you locate a flyway that is being used, you should build yourself a blind for concealment. The blind can be made of camo netting or pine boughs, or some combination of the two. Both have their advantages and disadvantages. The pine boughs make for a more substantial blind that offers more cover, and they do not tend to flap unnaturally in the wind as does the light camouflage cloth. On the other hand, the boughs dry out and lose their color and the needles fall out. Also, they are heavy to drag around and require more energy to cut and erect.

Camo netting, though expensive, is lightweight and reusable almost forever. It can be carried handily and easily in the game-coat pocket so that you can use almost any area to make a blind. Actually, the best blinds are combinations of the two materials—boughs of some type trimmed and finished off with the netting.

The blind should be erected before it is used, so that the crows can become a bit accustomed to it and so that no noise and commotion occurs on the day of the hunt. The blind should be about a quarter of a mile (400 yards or so) off the main flyway. The idea is to lure several crows at a time off the flyway and over your blind for shooting. If you stake out your blind right on the flyway and then shoot into the major flock of crows, you will quickly teach these canny birds to change their flight pattern and go elsewhere. This means you will have to start all over again.

On the other hand, if you lure them over your blind in twos,

Crows are wary and hard to lure within shotgun range, but leaving dead ones on the ground to call more in doesn't seem to deter them. (Photo courtesy of James R. Olt)

threes and small groups of up to ten or twelve, you will get far more shooting. When the crows learn about your blind, you merely shift location farther down the flyway and to the other side without making the crows completely change their flights. This means more shooting for you with less lost time to locate where the birds are flying.

Overcast, stormy and windy days always seem better for crow shooting. Perhaps this is because they have to fly farther for food. No one is exactly sure why, but these are the days when there is usually more flight activity and more sport. The morning flight has always, in my experience, been about three times as productive as the evening flight (though I have had some fine sport on the late flight at times). You should be in your blind ready for action about dawn. The flight (and the sport) may keep up for as long as sixty to ninety minutes, depending upon how many crows are flying and how many of them are migrants who haven't learned about your blind and the shooting in this area.

An owl decoy usually increases our action about 100 percent. If the owl decoy is a mounted owl skin (check the legality of this in your area), it works about twice as well as even the best paper-composition owl figures. The latter, however, erected on top of a 20-foot pole or placed in the top of a small tree where it can be seen at long range by the crows, helps a lot. Crows hate owls with a passion bordering on the unbelievable because the latter kill many of them at night when they are helpless. During the day the raucous and aggressive crows will mob any owl they can find in order to try and drive it out of their territory.

We always try to position our blind so that the wind is blowing *into* our faces. When the crows come to the call and the owl decoy, they invariably circle around to come into the wind toward the owl. Thus, if you are facing into the wind, the crows will circle around and come into the decoy from *behind* you. This gives you several advantages. First, the crows approach from your rear and are not as likely to spot you. The hardest part of yourself to camouflage is your face, and it's not so noticeable when they come from the back. Also, when they come from behind you and pass over you, they will be feathering down to a slow, almost stalling speed as they pass above you. (Your blind

197

A great horned owl decoy of one type or another will more than double your crow-hunting success when placed in an elevated and clearly visible position.

should be about 40 to 50 feet from both the decoy and the speaker of your electronic caller.) This means that you have your best shots as they pass over and in front of you because they are flying at their slowest and looking away from you toward the decoy.

We have also found that it is best to erect several blinds along more than one flyway. Crows are smart and, for birds, seem to possess a remarkable memory. We like to rest a blind for at least two weeks, preferably three, before using it again, if we have shot it over pretty thoroughly. Thus, if we are hunting crows twice a week, we like to have at least four different blinds to work so that we don't shoot the same blind too often. Otherwise the black bandits *learn* too quickly, and your shooting from a given blind is over after about the second time you make good use of it.

Basic equipment for this sport is simple. An owl decoy can be had for a reasonable price at almost any sporting-goods store. The same goes for camo clothing, gloves and face mask (or camo cream like that often used by archers and turkey hunters) and a mouth-blown crow call. An electronic call can also be a big help if you plan to pursue this sport much. You can turn it to a louder volume than you can blow a mouth call and it doesn't tire you out from long usage. Also, a cassette game caller (which I prefer to the bulkier record-playing types) can help you perfect

An electronic caller is not necessary for good crow-hunting success. Crows are raucous, loud-mouthed birds and much easier to call in than ducks or geese or wily predators like foxes, coyotes or bobcats. An inexpensive mouth call such as this is fine for the beginner . . . along with a bit of practice against a training record or cassette. (Photo courtesy of Johnny Stewart)

199

your mouth-calling talents. A variety of crow-calling sounds are available, and at one time or another all can be effective. The crow-in-distress or dying-crow call, however, seem to be more effective more often than the owl call, the crows-fighting-an-owl-or-hawk call, or the various other calls.

When you do get some shooting from a blind, don't worry about picking up any fallen crows. Leave them on the ground. They don't seem to interfere with things anyway. Usually after you shoot the first couple of times, those crows that you don't hit are long gone (unless you wound a crow which lures them back). But if you don't reveal yourself, you may be able to call a new batch out of the next group coming down the flyway a few minutes later.

Most any repeating shotgun will do, in either 12 or 20 gauge. Crows are not usually shot at long range and aren't hard to knock down. They are not as large as they seem, nor are they as tight-feathered and armor-plated as some of the ducks and geese. We use low-base (standard velocity) number 7½ or number 8 shot and find that does perfectly well for them. The thing about crows is that usually they will be a hundred yards or more out of range or, if you've done your job properly with blind, decoy and calling, they'll be right on top of you!

LONG-DISTANCE RIFLE SHOOTING AT CROWS

Though the quarry is the same, the name of the game is completely different. Here you cruise back-country roads until you spot crows feeding in a field or sitting in trees. Then, depending upon state laws about how closely you are allowed to shoot from secondary roads and/or vehicles, you shoot at them from long distance with an extremely accurate, flat-shooting rifle.

This is no sport for the casual shooter. The average deer rifle won't cut it here. A flat-shooting .22 centerfire (preferably one of the hotter ones like the .22/250 or the .220 Swift) or perhaps a hot .24- or .25-caliber gun wearing at least a 6x scope is called for. Actually, a 10x or stronger scope really comes into its own here.

200

Although crows are wary, they are not especially difficult to bring down. Standard-velocity shotgun shells with number 7½ or number 8 shot will do nicely. (Photo courtesy of James R. Olt)

Also required are a good pair of binoculars of at least 8x and a good spotting scope of 20x or more. It is often necessary to glass great expanses of rolling farm country from a high vantage point to locate crows or likely looking areas for crows and then approach them either by vehicle or on foot. It's a good idea to carry around a sandbag or two for a solid rest that you can assume, placed over the hood of your vehicle (if pulled off the road and far enough into a field to comply with local and state laws) or over a large rock or fence. Never shoot with your rifle's forearm resting on anything hard. Barrel vibrations rebounding from the hard rest will throw your point of impact off far too much for this kind of precision shooting.

Be extremely careful when shooting at crows sitting in trees. Many of these flat-shooting guns have a theoretical maximum range approaching or exceeding two miles when fired at an angle of roughly 37 degrees. This is just about the angle that some of your longish shots at crows sitting in a high tree on a hillside above you might be. Always be sure there is a backstop for your bullet when firing at a crow in a tree. Don't take a chance of wounding people or livestock several fields away.

This is much more specialized and demanding sport than most any other rifle shooting. The target is far smaller than it looks (skin out or pluck a crow sometime and look at that small-fist-sized body—you'll be quite surprised), the shots are long, and tricky wind currents you don't even know about from your shooting point may be eddying around out there.

You'll doubly earn every "blackie" you hit this way. But either way, whether you use shotgun or rifle, don't worry about wiping out the crow population anytime soon. Like foxes and coyotes, these are extremely wary, intelligent and adaptable animals that have already proven not only that they can take everything man can throw at them and survive but that they can prosper, extending both their range and numbers!

13

Anyone for Year-round Bird Hunting?

We shivered behind the big silo at the end of the barn, ears burning in the February wind. Suddenly Don's voice sounded off from the other side of the rambling barn. "Three on the right!"

Almost before the words registered enough for me to make the association that birds were coming over my side of the barn, three chunky pigeons zoomed forward and then flared away as they caught sight of me. I stepped out from the silo and raised the 12-gauge while the birds did a pigeon's version of the Immelmann turn that would have made the Red Baron blush with shame.

I didn't ruffle a feather on the first shot, and by then the first two had doubled back over the barn toward Don. The third one made the mistake of dawdling a bit, and I did manage to fold him up cleanly in one shot. While my bird was still plummeting to the ground, I heard Don get into action over on the other side of the barn.

As I walked over to pocket my bird, Stan and Ted joined me. They had staked out my end of the barn over to the left, but neither had had a clear shot as the birds had broken my way. Then I saw Don headed toward us with another of the slate-blue birds in his hand. Two out of three. On pigeons that's not bad in anyone's book, and since we were all turning a bit slate-blue from the cold ourselves, we headed for the warm basement of Don Martz's farmhouse and our ritual coffee break.

We were hunting the fast-flying, fancy-stepping "city pigeon" (or "barn pigeon") that is common throughout practically the entire country and that has reached pest proportions on most farms surrounding our cities. These pigeons make a challenging target and can provide year-round sport. Far too many sportsmen are missing out on good shooting—and good eating—right in their own backyards. And almost any farmer will welcome you with loud cries of joy and open arms if you convince him that you will *safely* shoot his pigeons.

PIGEONS AND DOVES

Pigeons are merely large-sized doves. Or, to put it another way, doves are merely small-sized pigeons. The birds come from the same family and the terms are used practically interchangeably even by the experts, with "dove" implying the smaller members and "pigeon" implying the larger. Even the authorities can't seem to agree on where one leaves off and the other begins. No matter. They're all sporting birds that are good to eat.

It's amazing that even though mourning doves are our single most hotly pursued game bird or animal today, with more shots being fired and more birds being grassed, practically no one hunts the common pigeon. This is even more remarkable when you consider that the passenger pigeon, another close relative, was the most hotly pursued game bird in the history of mankind. (Incidentally, it was not sport hunting that eradicated the bird!) Although even the crow now enjoys protective season regulations, to my knowledge there are no bag limits or season limits of any kind placed on the pigeon anywhere in the country. Pigeons have grown to be such pests that they don't need any such protection.

Pigeons are interesting birds. They were domesticated as early as the fifth Egyptian dynasty, some five thousand years ago, and are mentioned throughout the Bible in numerous contexts. Over two hundred strains of the domestic pigeon exist today, and it is believed that all are descended from this single species of rock dove *(Columba livia)* that we are all so familiar with.

In recent years this city dweller became so thick in many

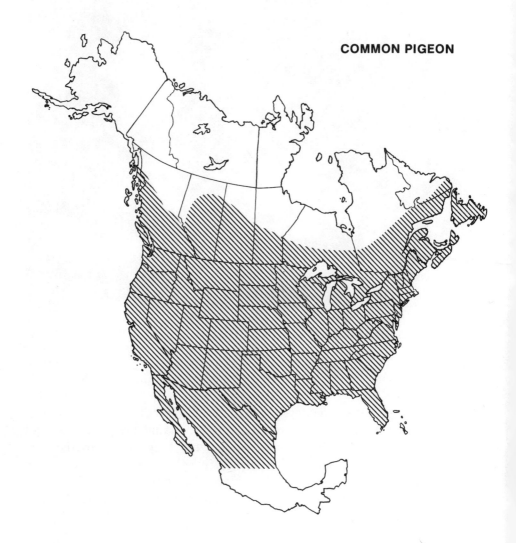

COMMON PIGEON

The common barn or city pigeon is a fast-flying, sporty, and tasty target that is neglected by all too many small game hunters. (Photo by Leonard Lee Rue, Jr.)

cities that it started moving farther and farther out into the country. First, large flocks would be unable to find adequate food and water in the city, so they would wing their way into the surrounding farmlands each morning (pigeons and doves are among the fastest of all birds, which is why they make such sporty pass-shooting targets) and then return to city roosts in the evenings. Then "city" pigeons began to establish permanent populations in the country and became known as "barn" pigeons. As these domestic or semi-domesticated pigeons reverted to the wild (and you'll find just how wild and wily they can be when you start trying to shoot them), it became the fashion among ornithologists and other bird-knowledgeable folk to refer to them by their wild-species name, the rock dove.

206

Originally this bird inhabited Europe, Central Asia and China in the wild state. Though no one seems to know exactly when they were introduced into this country, there is no doubt that these big 11-inch-long chukar-sized birds have become a major farmland pest, costing farmers hundreds of millions of dollars a year. They breed prolifically, all year round in those areas with light winters. They mature rapidly in only four weeks and eat tremendous amounts of wheat, corn, peas and most all the cereal grains and seeds that the farmers depend on for their own well-being. More times than not even the legendary peregrine falcon could not catch one in level flapping flight without the benefit of a high-altitude stoop.

HUNTING PIGEONS

We hunt these big-breasted speedsters several ways and often employ most methods on a single hunt. Pigeons stick to certain somewhat changeable but roughly predictable flight patterns. They water and feed in the mornings and afternoons, and if you keep up with their movements on specific farms (or better yet, ask the farmer to do so and call you) you usually know their current movements and can set up quick-and-rough cornstalk blinds for some nice pass shooting. This pass shooting usually doesn't last long—only about twenty to thirty minutes on a good flight—but if you have large pigeon populations in the area, you'll get some fast shooting excitement during that time.

Although we sometimes build blinds out of hastily gathered branches and twigs or dried cornstalks, most often we stake out a simple blind of camo cloth or netting that we also use when shooting crows. (Incidentally, a good crow shoot can often be combined with a pigeon hunt during the right time of year.) Early in the morning and late in the afternoon are the best times for this fly-by shooting, and if you're lucky you'll get a bit of shooting both as they're coming and as they're going.

Although we have tried jump-shooting pigeons, we've never found this to be very rewarding. Most people whose only exposure to these birds has been in the city, where they practically

207

had to kick them out from underfoot in order to walk on the sidewalk, are greatly surprised at how wary these country pigeons get as they revert more and more to the wild state. You can't often walk to within good shotgun range. They usually won't hold well enough, or at least not in the East, where I've done most of my pigeon potting.

There is another very productive method, however, which works particularly well during cold weather. The birds tend to flock together more and stick closer to their warm nests in the barns and other farm outbuildings. What we do in periods like this is take turns playing "bird dog" to flush them out. We flip a coin to see who'll be the "dog" to start out and then we rotate afterward.

As we approach each building where we know there are birds, the "dog" openly walks up to the barn or building from the most open side. The others have already circled around and sneaked up on the other three sides, employing all possible natural or man-made cover (silos, farm implements, wagons, etc.) to mask their approach.

If the "dog" is making enough commotion, the birds' attention will be riveted on him and invariably, right before he gets within shotgun range, they'll flush out in the opposite direction, right over the position of one or more crouching hunters at the other side of the barn. The "dog" usually tries to call out how many birds are breaking and which way ("Three at two o'clock!"), so that the others have at least a split second of warning before those jet-assisted targets come hurtling into sight from behind the barn. This calls for fast snap shooting, and no one needs to worry about exterminating the pigeon population!

It's better to have two to four hunters, rather than only one, picketed out at several spots around the far side of the barn. Although the birds usually flush in the general direction away from the "dog," they are often angling out in one direction or another, and a single hunter would not be able to cover enough territory. Thus much good shooting would go a-begging.

Also, a good barrage of shots will in many cases turn some of the birds back the way they came so that the hunter playing "dog" can get in a shot or two. This reminds me of similar

208

A combination rifle/shotgun model such as this Savage Model #2400, featuring a 12-gauge shotgun barrel and a .222 rifle barrel, is a good choice when out on a combination woodchuck-crow-pigeon "pest safari" during the off season for other same game. (Photo courtesy of SAVAGE ARMS CO.*)*

behavior I've seen on large mourning-dove shoots in the South, where many hunters may ring a field to which the doves come to feed. If they are lucky enough and send up a big enough barrage, the birds will often wheel around the field in two or three complete turns, giving everyone extra shooting. I have even been on pigeon shoots where we had enough hunters to have two "dogs," and between them they were able to turn several birds of a large flock back still again for a second pass over the hunters crouching at the far end. That's when the action gets super-heated!

On a good day, several hunters can usually shoot two dozen or more birds, if they keep up with pigeon roost locations and flight patterns. We use high-based 12-gauge number 6 shot to ground these robust thick-feathered birds properly. They're tougher to bring down than a mourning dove.

Though this shooting is a secondary brand of sport (and I'm not comparing it with more orthodox types of upland bird gunning), it is a nice off-season way to extend your hunting and get out into the field more. Shooting out a farmer's excess pigeons is often a good way to get his approval for more classic small game hunting during the fall season. By the way, these pigeons are excellent in the pot. I prefer them to mourning doves and I have friends who swear (sacrilege!) that they're better than bobwhite or pheasant.

209

PART IV
After the Hunt Is Over

14

How to Clean and Dress Your Small Game

There is a classic anecdote about eating wild meat in which Person A (who can alternatively be another hunter, a nonhunter or a housewife) tells Deer-hunting Person B, "You know, I just can't stand venison. I've tried deer meat time and again over the years and I just don't seem to have a taste for it."

To which stalwart Deer Hunter B inquires, "Do you like prime-grade beef?"

"Sure."

"All right. Do you think you'd like it quite as well if someone shot the steer several times and then let it run for a quarter of a mile before it died, pumping adrenaline, rather than killing it cleanly? Then, after that, suppose they tied it over the fender or on top of the car and drove several hundred miles home with it drying out in the wind and collecting all sorts of road dust and dirt? And then, after they arrived home, suppose they did an indifferent job of cleaning the meat, butchering it so badly that it ended up in unrecognizable and unappetizing-looking chunks? And then if they wrapped it badly, not sealing it tightly against freezer burn and slow-froze it (rather than quick-freezing it) so that much of the flavor was lost? If it was handled in that sort of slipshod fashion, and then overcooked and served carelessly at the table, just how much do you think you'd enjoy *beef?*"

"Hmmmm. Never thought of it quite like that!"

It's an old story but there's a lot of truth in it, and fully as much for the small game hunter as for the deer hunter, because what the small game hunter is bringing home is also inevitably going to be compared with professionally cleaned, dressed and wrapped poultry or meat.

Wild game has a unique, tangy flavor that I for one prefer to most bland and fatty domestic meats. It has more character and taste than the chemically fortified slabs found in the super-market—*if* you do your part by killing the game cleanly, dressing it promptly and correctly and freezing it properly. Other things being equal, wild game is *better* than today's overly fat, overly fortified, overly rationalized foodstore-chain meats. Follow the directions in this section and you'll agree with me.

THE BASICS OF DRESSING ANY SMALL GAME

Though the vast majority of small game shot and eaten by the public consists of cottontail rabbits and gray squirrels, there are some basics that apply to the proper care of any small game meat afield.

1. *Field dress the game as soon as possible after the kill.* By field dressing we primarily mean opening the body cavity and cleaning out all the viscera. In some cases this can also include removing the head, feet or hide. But the main thing is to get those quick-spoiling intestines out of there as rapidly as possible—especially on warm days or with game that is killed early during an all-day hunt and thus will be carried around most of the day next to your own warm body.

2. *Carry plastic bags.* Game pockets of hunting coats in-evitably accumulate dirt and debris in them. Carrying handy, sealable plastic bags protects your game from drying out as well as from dirt, and this is especially important if you have removed the hide when you emptied the body contents. Carry enough bags to pack each animal separately so that skinned meat isn't rubbing directly against unskinned animals.

214

3. *When dressing animals, do not get hair on the meat.* Always avoid getting hair on your hands and then transferring it to the meat. Not only is this unsightly (if hairs are left on the meat to be found later during cooking or eating), this is where the "wild" taste comes from. Some hunters wear gloves when dressing their game and others just get the knack, after a bit of practice, of keeping the carcass clean of hair.

4. *Use kitchen shears as well as a knife for cleaning game.* Shears are far handier than a knife for most small game cleaning operations, whether at home or afield, yet surprisingly few sportsmen use them. Shears make taking the heads and feet off small game animals a convenient and clean operation.

5. *Dress all game yourself, preferably out of sight of non-hunters.* Leaving the chore of dressing the game to nonhunting family members isn't very smart or very fair. Sure, if the kids want to help out and it's fun for them, by all means let them do so. But never draft anyone into doing this for you. You shot the game, and it's your responsibility to clean and care for it.

Better yet, you should do this out of sight of nonhunters. When a "poultry-counter-clean" small game parcel is seen by a nonhunter, it is attractive and appetizing looking. But exposing a person who never sees meat except at the supermarket to any of the necessary cleaning operations may detract from the enjoyment of the meat later. Of course, the commercially processed poultry, beef and pork they have been eating all their lives went through essentially the same operations to get to the market, but they just aren't used to *seeing* it happen.

6. *Check each dressed carcass for wounds.* If there are any spots under the skin where blood was collected from a wound, slice through the dark area to let out the small amount of blood and then wash that area thoroughly. Use the point of your knife to check out any small wounds and thus coax out as much of the bird shot you peppered the game with as possible. You will inevitably miss a few of these, and someone may "find" a number 6 shot when chewing the game later. There's nothing

wrong or even distasteful about this, it's just a bit annoying. Removing all the shot possible during the cleaning of the game is simply the best idea.

7. *Before cooking, soak freshly cleaned game in salt water for several hours*. This helps remove any potential "wild" taste and takes out any bloodstains that may be present around wound areas. I usually soak my game overnight in the refrigerator with a plate or saucer resting over the game so that it is kept *submerged* in the brine. The strength of the brine doesn't matter too much. Three or four heaping tablespoonsful of salt are adequate for a large bowl holding the cut-up parts of two or three cottontails.

If you are going to freeze the meat, however, do not soak it first. The soaking should always be done just before cooking.

CLEANING COTTONTAIL RABBITS

There is a quick and easy way to gut rabbits that requires no knife or other tools and is much cleaner than other methods. Merely turn the rabbit over so that its belly is up with the head toward you and clasp both hands firmly around the midsection immediately in back of the ribs and at the front of the abdomen. Squeeze very tightly and "walk" both hands backward toward the rabbit's tail. As you do this, the rabbit's viscera or intestines will ball up and collect at the back end of the abdominal cavity. When you have this ball collected, lay the rabbit's back against the ground, keeping the pressure on this tightly balled mass with one hand (so it can't disperse), and push hard against the top of this ball with the knotted fist of your other hand—a quick, strong shove. This will force the soft-skinned stomach covering to rupture and all the viscera (or about 95 percent of it anyway) will be forced out.

With a bit of practice, this takes about ten seconds to perform. You don't need anyone's help or even the help of a knife or other implement. Later, at home, you will want to open up the belly cavity and fine-dress the rabbit, but this method will see you through most of it in the field. Best of all, you can do this without soiling your hands or getting any hair on the meat or inside the body cavity. Actually, with this easy method there is no excuse for not immediately field dressing all rabbits in order to maintain maximum flavor. (Since squirrels are smaller, built differently and much more "thick-skinned," this method doesn't work with them.)

Finish dressing the rabbit at home by opening the body cavity thoroughly and cleaning out any remaining matter. Then take the head and feet off by using either heavy-duty kitchen or garden shears or a hatchet (for some unexplained reason most people try to do it the hard way with a knife). With either implement, the job can be done much more quickly and cleanly than with even the sharpest and largest of knives.

Once the head and feet are off, it's time to skin your rabbit, if you haven't already done so in the field. Actually, skinning in the field has its pros and cons. If it's extremely hot weather and you have plastic bags to protect the meat, it's often a good idea to skin afield. Do not seal the bags tightly so that the meat gets rancid. If it's colder weather, I often wait and do it at home.

Whenever you do the skinning, it's easily accomplished with rabbits. After the head and feet are taken off, make a single cut *across,* not down, the back. Just cut through the skin, not deeply enough to slice into the meat itself, catch each side of this cut with a hand and pull your hands apart, thus shucking the skin right off in one easy, fluid movement. Since rabbits are so loose-skinned, this is simple to accomplish.

There is always a very thin, somewhat translucent membrane that stretches over most of a rabbit's backsides and down onto the hind legs. I always strip this off, since I think doing so improves both the taste and the appearance of the meat.

Now it's time to wash off the meat thoroughly. It's a good idea to use a stiff-bristled kitchen scrub brush to take off any stubbornly adhering hairs that are stuck to the meat.

The final operation is to cut the rabbit into pieces if desired. When planning to serve the rabbit in the next day or so, without freezing, I usually cut it up at this time. If we are freezing the meat and not planning to serve it in the near future, I will sometimes leave the rabbit whole.

There are two special conditions to be aware of when cleaning rabbits. The first is *tularemia,* a rare but potentially serious disease also sometimes known as "rabbit fever." Any rabbit that appeared lethargic and not alert when flushed, or that acted in any unusual manner, should be discarded and not kept (preferably burned or buried).

Rabbits that look and act healthy can conceivably also have this affliction; if so, their liver will be speckled with many pinhead-sized white spots. Any rabbit that has not acted normally should never be handled with your bare hands, especially if you have any cuts or abrasions there, since the parasite caus-

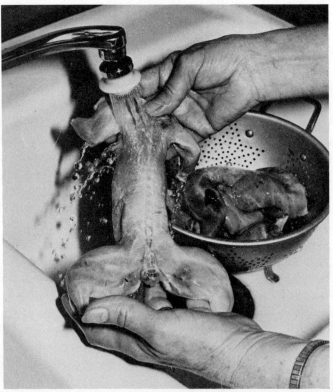

A final wash of this squirrel carcass can be done in the kitchen sink, but all other dressing and cleaning operations on small game should be done outside the kitchen.

218

ing the disease can enter the human body through open cuts and sores.

Some rabbit hunters take the precaution of always wearing gloves when cleaning bunnies. Sometimes I use gloves and sometimes I don't. To put this whole thing into perspective: though tularemia is a serious disease, fewer people are killed by it each year than by bee stings. And the newer mycin-type drugs are very effective against the disease. I have handled hundreds of rabbits over the years and have never had the disease or even known anyone who had it. Even so, it's something to be aware of and guard against, especially if the rabbit appeared sick. Wear gloves if you have them handy, but don't let the remote possibility of tularemia rob you of some of the best wild eating there is!

The second thing to be aware of is that cottontails, like the larger and farther-north caribou, are also plagued by *botflies,* which lay their eggs under rabbit fur. When the larvae hatch, they burrow under the rabbit's skin and develop there.

As these larvae grow, they cause large lumps under the skin, often back toward the hindquarters of the rabbit. These are variously called "warbles," "wools," "woofs" or "wolves" in different regions of the country. They are most prevalent during the warm months of late summer and early fall.

Though these growths do not affect either the taste or the safety with which you can handle and eat the meat, many hunters find them distasteful. One way to avoid them is to wait until after the first hard frost and cold weather begins in earnest. The first freeze usually kills any rabbits much affected by these pesky parasites. If it doesn't kill the rabbits, then it will kill the parasites themselves, solving the problem one way or the other. Do not confuse these parasites with tularemia, incidentally. The two have nothing to do with each other.

CLEANING GRAY SQUIRRELS

The method for cleaning gray squirrels is very similar to that for cleaning rabbits, with the following exceptions.

You must use a knife to gut a squirrel. The "milking" technique recommended for rabbits won't work with tight-bodied tree squirrels. Cut through the belly skin, taking care not to cut too deeply and into the entrails themselves. Then sling out most of the entrails, cleaning out the rest with your hands. Try to avoid getting hair on the meat. Wearing gloves can help, even though tularemia isn't a factor.

Taking the head and feet off squirrels is more difficult than with rabbits. A hatchet is easiest, and even shears are better than a knife.

Skinning squirrels is much tougher than skinning rabbits. Make the back cut well around the animal (but avoid slicing down into the meat) and try to jerk more strongly and abruptly with your two hands when shucking or "unzipping" the hide from the animal. Actually, two sportsmen can work on this, with one using both hands to pull one side of the cut and the other using both hands on the other side (twice the horsepower, so to speak). Sometimes cutting a small hole through a flap of the skin for a better handhold can help a lot. This is where it's all too easy to get squirrel hair on the meat—and once on, it's the devil's own task getting it off!

After your squirrel is skinned, always be sure to cut away the small kernel of brownish-yellow fat in the "armpit" under the forelegs. Though failure to do this won't ruin the taste outright, it certainly does degrade it. These two kernels are some sort of musk glands and should be excised very carefully. Cut widely and deeply around them, so that you don't rupture them while taking them out. Be careful not to touch them with your hands and then touch the meat.

Be sure to scrub the meat diligently with a brush. Squirrel hairs are much easier to get onto the meat and much tougher to get off than rabbit hairs. Also, they degrade the taste more. Take your time. Look the carcass over carefully under a good light and clean the meat thoroughly under running water.

CUTTING UP RABBIT AND SQUIRREL

Both animals are cut up in exactly the same fashion, and each yields five or six pieces of meat, depending upon whether

220

Squirrels are more difficult to skin than rabbits. They should be cut crosswise across the back (just through the skin not into the meat) and then "shucked" vigorously, with a hand grasping each side of the cut. Jerk strongly and abruptly, and it's not so hard to unzip old bushy-tail!

you elect to keep one marginal piece or throw it away. This is a matter of personal preference, and since the piece (as we'll explain) is so bony, it's not really a matter of wasting good meat.

First, cut off the back legs of the rabbit or squirrel much as you would when dressing a deer or other animal. The difference is that the rabbit or squirrel can be disjointed with a knife, but here again kitchen shears are much quicker and cleaner to use.

221

After removing both hind legs, remove the front legs. This leaves you with a single long piece, the central (or backbone) portion of the carcass.

At this stage I always cut away the loose skin that wrapped around and enclosed the belly. There is no meat or substantial eating here, and trimming away these loose, ragged-looking flaps of skin makes for a far neater, more professionally dressed portion. (No small thing when nonhunters will be sampling your wild game and are used to seeing only professionally processed meat!)

This long backbone portion should now be cut in two immediately behind the ribs. The back portion (or saddle) is actually the meatiest and most tender part of the animal. The front piece is almost all bone, consisting only of the ribs and overback section joining the ribs. Many throw this portion away. If I elect to keep it, I usually trim about half an inch or so off the rib ends (sawing them a bit with a heavy knife or clipping them with those ever-handy shears) in order to keep only the meatiest part.

FINAL HINTS ON CLEANING ANY GAME

Always clean your game outside if at all possible. Messing up the family kitchen is not a way to endear yourself and your hunting pastime to the nonsporting members of your household. When working outside, always make sure that you have a well-lit area in which to work. (This final cleaning process usually ends up taking place at night.) Working without being able to see well usually ensures cut hands and badly dressed meat. Besides, it's just uncomfortable, unattractive and easily avoided by a bit of forethought.

Always have your tools at hand. Sounds automatic, eh? Maybe so, but many sportsmen seem to sweep up a few things quickly and almost as an afterthought, and then when they are well into cleaning they discover they don't have the sharpening stone handy, or a small knife as well as a large one, or enough newspaper, foil or plastic wrap.

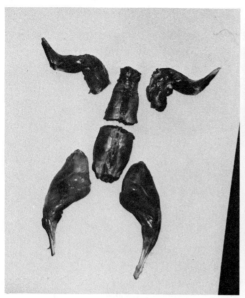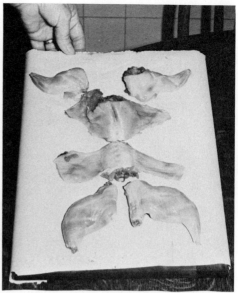

A cottontail rabbit properly sectioned for cooking (left). The best piece of all is the lower center saddle, followed by the meaty rear legs. The front legs have some meat on them, but the upper center or rib section is often thrown away. If it is to be kept, trim away the loose flaps of skin and cut off the rib ends as shown for neater, easier-to-store pieces.

A squirrel (right) should be sectioned into pieces about the same way. Here the flaps of skin and rib ends have not been trimmed off the upper and lower center pieces.

Always dispose of the waste matter so that it's not lying around in plain sight and so that it doesn't get a bit high if the garbage isn't picked up for a while and the weather is warm. A garbage disposal will handily take care of most anything you should reasonably come up with, and then it's gone once and for all. Otherwise bag it securely in plastic and place it in the garbage can.

Cleaning your game promptly and properly and without offending more tender sensibilities in the process makes all the difference. In fact, if you're a particularly cunning type, you'll even occasionally offer to cook the game dinner yourself. As any cook can tell you, the meal you don't have to prepare tastes best.

Make your small game dinners a treat. Cook them up and serve them yourself sometimes. You'll be amazed how much it helps, and it can even give you a bit of added satisfaction to do it up brown—from field all the way to platter in competent fashion.

15

Freezing Your Small Game for Better Taste

Freezing is an interesting and simple process, yet it's amazing how many otherwise knowledgeable people know so little about it. We'll cover a number of basics here that will help you improve the freezer life and taste of *everything* you keep in your refrigerator freezer or larger chest or upright home freezer, easily and conveniently.

About the only distinction between game and most other meats is that game is a bit drier and thus should be wrapped even more carefully to avoid undue drying out in the freezer. Actually, other things being equal, game should keep far better in the freezer than lamb, pork or seafood, and every bit as well as beef. But there are some tricks to make sure you get the most out of your frozen small game.

THE PROCESS OF FREEZING

Meat should be frozen as quickly as possible. Whenever any meat is frozen, ice crystals form inside the meat from the moisture that was in the meat itself. The faster the freezing process, the smaller these crystals are, with less resultant cellular damage. Whenever the meat is thawed, these crystals melt and the precious juices and oils of the meat—literally its *flavor*—are scattered and diluted. The quicker the freezing, the smaller these crystals and the less flavor loss due to dilution of these oils

225

and juices. This is why commercial packers and food lockers resort to ultra-fast "blast freezing" to lock in the flavor.

Though you cannot duplicate the capabilities of these industrial-grade freezers with your home unit, you can do everything to ensure the fastest possible freezing by not overloading the freezer with too much meat to be frozen at once. Also, place the meat to be frozen immediately on or next to the freezing coils or compressor in your freezer—in the coldest part of the freezer, in other words. If necessary, turn your freezer temperature down in order to accelerate this freezing, and do not keep opening and closing the door "to see how it's doing," thus letting out the precious cold.

One note: Although rapid freezing is vital, I don't particularly like to rush hot or warm meat right into the freezing process. Cool down your meat a bit in the refrigerator and then freeze it as quickly as possible.

People tend to talk about frozen meat "going bad." There is no black-and-white cutoff date after which "good" frozen meat suddenly "goes bad." The basic truth about freezing is that no meat is ever improved by it. There is a continual flavor deterioration. The trick is to minimize this flavor loss as much as possible and take it into consideration when preparing your meat after thawing it. Any meat that has been in the freezer a long time (over three or four months) should be prepared with spices and flavorings rather than broiled or cooked rare with no additional flavor helpers.

Bacteria are not killed by freezing. They're still lurking there in your meat, with their growth and reproduction largely arrested. Before we cover some specific tricks to help you do a better job on freezing your game (and other meats), let's do away with one old wives' tale. Almost everyone has heard it said that you should not ever refreeze anything once it has been frozen and thawed. Sometimes this statement is tendered on the basis of imminent food poisoning being the almost guaranteed result if someone is feckless enough to refreeze. Not so! Simple logic tells us why. If any meat is all right to eat at a given point in time, it is all right to refreeze. If you can't refreeze it, you'd better throw it away right then and there!

Game that has been frozen for long periods of time, and thus subject to flavor loss, can be boiled extensively until the meat scrapes easily away from the bone and then converted into tasty (and highly seasoned) soups or stews.

The *disadvantage* to refreezing and the reason it is not recommended is that this thawing and refreezing (even partial thawing and freezing again) is a severe flavor degrader. You are subjecting your meat to that ice-crystal buildup and then melt-down (when you later thaw it for the second time) an additional time, and this second cycle takes a severe toll of the flavor. The idea of freezing is *not* the avoidance of outright spoilage but the maximization of flavor retention. It's not hard to make the choice between dry, tasteless but edible meat and tasty, succulent meat dishes that bring us the tang of the outdoors many weeks later!

How long can frozen meat be kept? That's the most-asked question. It's sort of like the old "How long is a string?" question, because of the continual degradation in flavor, the many variables involved in keeping meat frozen properly and the varying acceptability of flavor loss among different people. However, a relative conservative estimate of storage life at varying temperatures, released by the American Meat Institute Foundation, is shown in the following table.

Storage Life of Frozen Meats (in Months)

	10 °F	0 °F	−10 °F	−20 °F
Beef	4	6	12	12 +
Lamb	3	6	12	12 +
Turkey/ Chicken	6	12	—	—
Pork	2	4	8	10
Veal	3	4	8	12

These figures assume that the meats were properly wrapped and protected during their freezer life. Note that the fattier meats have shorter freezer lives. Game meat would compare favorably with beef. The key fact shown by the table is that *the lower the temperature at which the meat is kept frozen, the less flavor it will lose.* Here are some tips to do a better job of protecting your tasty small game meat from the ravages of time in the freezer:

1. If you are not freezing your meat right away, thoroughly chill it within twenty-four hours after killing it. Ideal chill range is 33 to 36 degrees Fahrenheit, but it should be below 40 degrees in any event.

2. Keeping some game that may tend to be a bit tougher (older animals of the larger species) chilled for three to five days before freezing so that it "ages" a bit will improve its tenderness.

3. Do *not* freeze any animals stuffed with dressing. Always wait until thawing and final preparation before stuffing.

4. Drying out (or "freezer burn") is your main enemy. Wrap all meat thoroughly. Squeeze out all air from inside the package by "milking" it and then twisting the top of the freezer bag and sealing tightly. Use thicker, heavier-duty freezer bags that give more insulation and do not puncture as easily when meat is

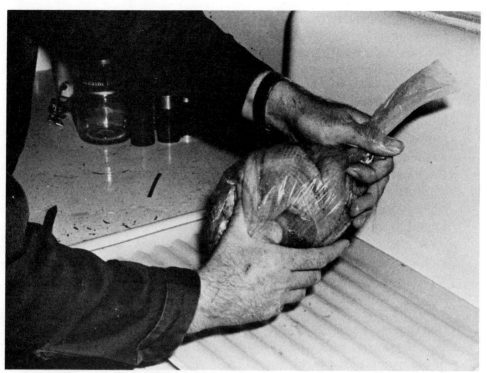

Before any meat is frozen, all air should be forced or "milked" out of the plastic bag or freezer wrap to approximate vacuum sealing as closely as possible. This greatly prolongs freezer life and means tastier eating whenever the meat is thawed and served.

handled and moved around in the freezer. Double-wrap those meat parcels that you think will be kept longer than six to eight weeks without thawing.

If possible, use one of the inexpensive home vacuum sealing units to package your game in. These small appliances (now available from Sears and most major small-appliance makers) use heavy-duty plastic and ensure that your packages are fully sealed and not subject to air leakage and drying.

5. Freeze your meat as quickly as possible by turning down freezer temperature controls and placing meat in the coldest spot in the freezer. A convenient rule of thumb is that a properly

functioning home freezer will adequately quick freeze at least two pounds of meat per cubic foot of freezer capacity up to a limit of about forty pounds. This varies a bit, with chest-type home freezers being considerably more efficient than uprights and full freezers being more efficient than empty or half-full ones. (That's right! The large amount of already hard-frozen food helps improve the insulation of the freezer and keep the temperature down, not the other way around.) And always remember that the more frequently you open the freezer door and the longer and wider you leave it open, the more you decrease your quick-freezing efficiency.

6. Consider freezing those items that you think will be kept frozen for extra-long periods of time in water inside a hard plastic container or even plastic-coated cardboard milk cartons. This method of freezing will take up more room, but it greatly increases the freezer life of your meat due to the added insulation.

7. Always check game to make sure that no broken bones are poking out to puncture the freezer bag or wrapping and let that dry cold air in to do its damage. If there are broken bones, trim the ragged ends with kitchen shears and tuck them back out of the way into the meat.

8. Label your meat parcels clearly as to contents and date frozen. Good freezer management—working on a first-in/first-out basis—ensures that you will get maximum flavor out of all your meat.

9. Avoid rough handling and rummaging around in your freezer. Those parcels may seem rock-hard, but if you puncture the thin wrapping you're going to greatly degrade flavor in short order!

10. If possible, *always cook thawed meat immediately for a minimum of flavor and texture loss.*

11. If you use the hard-plastic freezer containers, always buy the square-cornered ones rather than the rounded-corner or circular types. Square-cornered containers take up far less space and can increase the *bulk* (though not weight) storage capacity of your freezer by up to one third.

12. If possible, wrap and package your small game in meal-sized packets so you do not have to thaw more than you can use at one time.

230

As a general rule, the more fat there is on meat, the shorter its freezer life. Though most small game animals aren't overly fat, some raccoons and other species may be fatter than normal, especially if they have been eating a lot of corn. It's a good idea to trim this fat away before freezing. Not only does any fat shorten freezer life as a general rule, but game fat sometimes tends to impart a strong taste to the meat (as with lamb and mutton).

Bigger chunks of meat freeze better than smaller ones. To put it another way, the more surface area there is relative to weight or bulk, the quicker the meat tends to dry out in a freezer. Thus, stew meat won't keep as well as a large roast, or a whole small game animal will freeze a bit better than one that has been cut into parts. If you plan to cook your small game within a month or so, you may want to go ahead and cut it up into parts when dressing it and before freezing. I usually do. But if you want to keep it longer, it's often a good idea to freeze it whole unless it is too large for meal-sized packets. Also, though you will want to freeze most of your game in small quantities, you may want to freeze a few larger packages for meals when company comes or those "weekend-long" stews that taste so good during cold winter weather and seem to get better the second day you eat them.

The fact that larger pieces of meat freeze more efficiently is readily reflected in this American Meat Institute Foundation table comparing the freezer life of different cuts of beef from the same carcass.

BEEF	Months of Freezer Life
Ground meat	3–4
Stew meat	6–9
Steaks	6–12
Roasts	6–12+

Small game cut into pieces would compare with the stew meat, while whole animals would roughly parallel the steaks or roasts figures. But bear in mind again that meat toward the older end of the age range won't be as tasty as the "fresher" meat.

231

This should always be remembered when deciding how to cook and serve game. The older the game, the more you turn to the spice rack and the sauce recipes!

The single most common mistake home-freezer owners make is not knowing at what temperature they are running their freezer and not running it cold enough. How cold you need to run yours will vary, depending upon whether you have a chest or an upright, how much frozen meat you keep in it and how often it is opened. If you have a half-empty upright and several young children in your family, plan on running it 10 to 15 degrees colder than you would if you had a fully loaded chest-type freezer that is seldom opened and then closed quickly.

THE BIGGEST MISTAKE

Most home-freezer owners don't run their freezers cold enough. It's that simple. All too often these "freezers" are barely that, running at about 25 to 30 degrees Fahrenheit. True, most of the food is hard and frozen (except toughies like ice cream), but don't expect to keep meat flavorful very long under these conditions. Even in this era of spiraling energy costs, if you are using your freezer to keep substantial amounts of food frozen you will more than save the extra power costs of running it cold (down around 0 degrees Fahrenheit) by shopping for food in bulk during sales and at the best time of the year. The first thing to do is put a thermometer in the freezer and find out how cold it is in various sections. Then adjust the controls to ensure that it is running consistently at around 0 to plus 10 degrees Fahrenheit, and store your meat in the coldest area.

Remember that if the outside temperature is particularly hot, if your freezer is rather empty or if it is being opened more frequently than usual, you may have to lower the controls to keep it at the same desirable temperature. Check it periodically. You worked hard (though it was fun!) for that game and you shouldn't be robbed of its full enjoyment due to sloppy freezing techniques or bad freezer management. The rest of your food will taste better too, because domestic meats, vegetables, fruits and pastries will also remain fresher and more flavorful.

16

Trophies for the Small Game Hunter

On one wall of our family room I have a regal six-point bull elk head and a near-record moose head. Both are large and impressive. Across the way on the other wall hangs a nice, well-furred grizzly-bear rug, and throughout other rooms of the house are mountain goat, deer, caribou and a variety of other game trophies accumulated over a number of years spent in the field.

But I have other mementos—a nice well-furred coyote rug, a tanned snowshoe-rabbit hide, a montage of framed pictures from various small game hunts with my boys, to name a few. These are every bit as precious to me as the larger and more glamorous trophies, because the whole point is to help you recall special experiences more vividly as the years go by—not to impress others or yourself.

Though many would not think of associating trophies with small game hunting, there are certainly many possibilities for the creative and enterprising sportsman.

THE GAME ITSELF

The "big game" of small game lend themselves most readily to trophy consideration. Bobcats, coyotes, foxes and raccoons all make nice rugs if they are well furred. These rugs can be put up with a full mouth-open head mount or with the head not mounted. The former is much more expensive (usually about double the cost) but obviously makes for a nicer trophy. A nice

233

coon rug that can be used as a wall hanging or throw for the back of a chair or couch can be made up relatively inexpensively without a head mount.

When taking any of these trophies for a rug or life-sized mount, it is far better to let the taxidermist skin the animal—

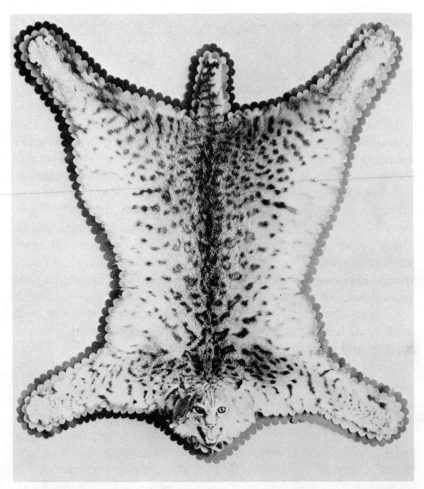

A well-furred bobcat rug with a full, open-mouth head mount makes a distinctive trophy for any den or family room. (Photo courtesy Jonas Brothers, Denver, Taxidermists)

234

especially around the delicate and difficult facial areas such as the eyes, nostrils and lips—than to attempt doing it yourself. For instance, it's surprising how much more lifelike any animal looks with the eyelashes on rather than trimmed off. Yet if you don't know what you're doing, it's extremely difficult not to lose one or both of these delicate appendages while handling and skinning the head. Nor should you gut the animal as if you were dressing it for the table. That's just one more large cut that may not meet the taxidermist's specifications for your mount, and in this case you are not trying to preserve the meat for the table.

First, inspect your trophy carefully and take off all blood spots with a dry rag or some grass. If necessary, use a bit of water. Try to wipe all blood from around the mouth or nostrils, and do not carry the animal in a head-down position, which might cause blood to accumulate there on the way out of the field. The best thing to do is leave the field as soon as possible and take the animal directly to a nearby taxidermist if feasible. While transporting the animal, do not leave it in a hot, dry car trunk or in the back of a car sitting in the direct sun with all windows rolled up so that an oven effect is created.

If you are not able to go directly to the taxidermist, smooth down all the fur of the animal, wrap it well in plastic garbage bags and store it in your freezer or that of a friend. If the frozen carcass isn't injured by rough handling in the freezer, it is perfectly possible to keep an animal in satisfactory condition for mounting for several years. (I once knew a fellow who kept a fox for seven years and then had an entirely satisfactory mount made!) You are not trying to keep the animal in edible condition but just to protect the fur from undue drying out and from freezer burn.

The skull of any of these larger small game animals makes a nice little memento itself. Even if you are having the trophy mounted, the taxidermist usually will not (should not, in fact) use the real skull. Plastic or paper-composition head forms with plastic teeth last far longer; real teeth always eventually crack and tend to come out of the sockets.

Thus, always ask the taxidermist to save the skull for you when preparing your mount. You can have the skull treated,

Here a hunter has had a large rock chuck (perhaps the product of a spectacularly long and difficult shot?) mounted for him. Small game trophies come in all types and sizes. (Photo courtesy of Jonas Brothers, Denver, Taxidermists)

perhaps bleached out for you, and then you can use it as a paperweight or piece of shelf memorabilia. Or you can have it mounted inexpensively on a wood plaque for wall hanging. If you

236

want to take the skull yourself rather than have a taxidermist do it, simply rough-skin it out and cook at a rolling boil for several hours to separate most of the meat from the skull. Then set it outside on the patio or porch to dry and weather. Small birds can pick out any remaining bits of dried meat adhering. Dust the skull with borax (Boraxo will do) to ensure that you are killing any pesky little mites or bugs. After a week or two of this simple "automatic" treatment, your skull is ready. If you want to bleach it whiter, treating it with a bit of peroxide (easily available from any drugstore) will do it.

Some parents have even had their child's first rabbit or squirrel mounted as a keepsake of when the youngster's lifetime of sport began. There are often apprentice taxidermists scattered around who do taxidermy work on a part-time basis. Though the quality of work can be variable, some is quite good. It's a good idea to tour some of these fellows' shops (often found in the basements of their homes) and look at their work for possible future reference. It's usually worth the extra cost to take a bobcat or coyote to a major taxidermy studio, but smaller mounts of animals like woodchucks, rabbits, squirrels and ground squirrels often can be put up quite reasonably and nicely by one of these part-time journeymen. This low-key approach can be especially intriguing when a sportsman takes an unusually colored animal (a black fox squirrel, for instance) or an unusually large specimen of one of the more common species. In this case the hunter may want to preserve the unique trophy but not want to spend a lot of money doing it.

Sometimes these apprentice taxidermists will even work up trades whereby if someone furnishes them a certain number of animals to practice on or mount for their own showroom display, they will do a free mount or two for that person. It's worth checking out in the off-season, so give it a try. At the least you'll meet some interesting people.

Taxidermists' shops are invariably fascinating places filled with all sorts of trophies and odds and ends. Taxidermists themselves are usually knowledgeable about the local sporting scene and good contacts to have in order to locate good areas to hunt or other sportsmen with similar interests.

A life-sized coyote makes an impressive small game trophy. This one is exhibited with a full museum-type background diorama. (Photo courtesy Jonas Brothers, Denver, Taxidermists)

PERSONALIZED MEMENTOS
THAT SERVE AS TROPHIES

Trophies are in the eye of the beholder. And that's oh, so true. A youngster's first shotgun shell fired at live game (or at *anything*) can be bronzed, or perhaps simply lacquered and attached to a small baseplate of wood that serves as a stand or a wall plaque. Candid photos of that first day afield could be attached to the baseplate to make a creative and personal memory refresher of an unforgettable day of fun and excitement (and humor, if the recoil of the big gun dumped the youngster with the first shot!).

Candid photos of small game outings can be used in an almost infinite variety of ways to make striking and yet inexpensive "trophies" that literally become priceless as the years roll by and the youngster featured so prominently in the pictures takes his or her own children and *their* children on some of their first small game hunts. These photos can be displayed informally under the glass of a desk or coffee table. They can be mounted in a montage on a nice piece of wood or perhaps framed with a burlap background. Of course, individual enlargements in 5 by 7, 8 by 10 or even 11 by 14 sizes can be matted and framed, when featuring particularly unique moments afield.

All sorts of keepsakes can be picked up from these small game jaunts, ranging from interesting rocks and mineral specimens to driftwood and dried pine cones. These can be used for everything from Christmas decorations and shelf bric-a-brac to the raw material that Mom uses in some of her arts and crafts projects. I even know one family that has a wall plaque that features hanging motel keys that have come from long-distance small game hunts they have made to other states. (They paid for the keys before taking them.)

Small game trophies are all around. They are anything and everything that help summon up, ever alive and bright, those memories of shared experiences when parents and children or hunting buddies were younger and the days afield were magical times.

APPENDIX I

How to Get Permission to Hunt on Other People's Land

Several states in the densely populated East have already passed the unenviable milestone of having 50 percent or more of their huntable land posted against hunting. That makes it tough to find a convenient place to hunt in some areas, but there are many things that thinking sportsmen can do to make sure they have good places to hunt where landowners welcome them back again and again.

Here are some down-to-earth tips that have worked for me over the years. Some are pretty basic and others may be new to you, but when you put them all together they'll go a long way toward ensuring that you always have good places to hunt.

1. *Always ask permission.* This one is so basic I almost skipped it. Then I remembered all the times I have heard various people say, "I would have asked but I didn't know where the house was," or, "They're probably not at home anyway," or, "We didn't want to disturb the landowner." Horsefeathers! If you don't have permission to hunt there, stay off the property. Any "reasons" for not asking are just an excuse.

You may be able to hunt there without permission the first time because the landowner didn't want to come out and throw you off his property right then and there. That doesn't mean anyone is getting away with anything, however. Next time you come by, the landowner will probably have taken the precaution of thoroughly posting his land against all trespassing and hunting. Then that land is lost to all of us hunters forever because of one person's bad manners.

2. *Approach the landowner's house properly.* I mean as if your sick grandmother were in the front room with a headache. I've seen a carload of hunters screech to a stop in front of a house and pile out making more noise than an infantry squad. Through all the bluster and horseplay it's a wonder the poor farmer can even understand what the one who was delegated to "go to the door" is trying to say to him. And then these types wonder why the answer is usually a resounding "No!"

3. *Approach the landowner himself properly.* Be polite. Try to have some insight into his problems and considerations in these matters. Approach him with goodwill rather than in a surly, foot-dragging manner that telegraphs your resentment at having to ask his permission. Believe me, the difference in the two attitudes shows.

4. *Ask him where you can hunt.* Rather than considering access to be a blanket option to go anywhere and hunt anywhere, get specific instructions about where you can (and cannot) go. Impress upon him your sincere interest in the safety of his livestock and equipment. Have a pencil and piece of paper handy in case he wants to draw you an informal map of the lay of the land.

5. *Ask about any rules he may have or want to lay down.* Some landowners would like you off their place by a certain hour. Others would appreciate it if you don't climb *over* any fences but rather go through them or through the gates (almost all want their gates closed). Again, it's his land, so impress upon him that you will abide by his rules.

6. *Tell him you will pick up and carry off all your empty shells.* The almost indestructible plastic shotshell has come into its own—much to the dismay of most farmers and ranchers. Far from biodegradable, these things simply will not rot away in a short time like the older paper shells. They are unsightly and can be dangerous if left lying around. In fast-action pursuits like dove shooting, rabbit rousting or crow hunting, you can litter the ground significantly in just a few moments. You carried them in loaded, you can sure carry them out empty! You don't want to bother with having to pick them all up and collect them? Then the farmer will eventually have to.

7. *Tell him you will pick up any carcasses and will not leave refuse from your cleaned game on his property.* Those mental giants who like to leave garlands of dead woodchucks or crows draped from every handy fence or gate sure aren't doing the rest of us any favors. These little signs of the hunter's "prowess" are definitely out of step with the times. They make the landowner mad and arouse just that much more anti-hunting sentiment from those nonhunters driving along the roads or walking the fields.

The same goes for dressing out the small game. Sure, you can dress it right in the field to preserve as much of the flavor and good taste as possible. But you can do it on the papers you brought along for such purposes and you can stuff the whole lot into a plastic leaf or trash bag and cart it back to your own garbage can.

8. *Show the landowner formal identification.* Let him know who you are. Show him your driver's license, social security card, or other basic I.D. Leave him your name, address and license number. That way he knows you are serious about all the fine things you have been saying about respecting his property and livestock. And he can get in touch with you and call any "mistakes" to your attention.

9. *Offer to leave a $25 security deposit.* Occasionally, in addition to properly identifying myself and proving I'm who I say I am, I also offer to leave (and sometimes do leave) a $25 deposit against any damage to the property. Of course, you get your money back when you leave after the hunt, but this offer can often convince the farmer, like nothing else, of your sincerity. You're literally putting your money where your mouth is.

10. *Tell him you will not bring (or refer) other hunters to his place.* The single most frequent complaint landowners have about hunters (and the reason more land is posted against hunting than any other) is that once they have given permission to one person to hunt, that hunter often seems to regard it not only as a blanket access permit for himself but also as the right to tell others about the place and bring them along. By the time the others start telling still others, the poor landowner begins to wonder where it will all end.

Assure the landowner that if he will let you (or the two or

three of you) hunt, you realize that that applies only to you or your group and only for today. Don't give him the feeling that he's mortgaging the place to fifty other fellows he's never seen. If he does give his permission, go back and ask him each time you want to hunt. It's his land, not yours, and that's the way you'd want it if the positions were reversed.

One final thought: Do a little something nice for him. Don't just take things for granted. He's doing something nice for you by allowing you the run of his place. Even things out a little. Offer to share some of your game (which you have already cleaned) with him, or perhaps an occasional box of shells or a small Christmas present would be appropriate. It shouldn't be anything out of scale, just a little remembrance here and there for his consideration. You'll find yourself with a permanent place to hunt and quite possibly a good friend you would not otherwise have had.

APPENDIX II

How to Introduce Your Youngster to Small Game Hunting

It's a well-known fact that youngsters aren't just scaled-down adults. Every parent should know this all too well. No, our children are different in kind as well as in dimension. And yet it's amazing how many well-meaning adults rather left-handedly try to introduce their youngsters to small game hunting with little or no forethought or special planning. That's a shame. It's so easy to do the thing correctly, and not to do so almost always spells failure in the form of a bored and restless child, an exasperated adult and an empty game bag. In extreme cases it can even occasionally result in a tragic accident that maims or kills.

Small game hunting is your youngster's ticket to a broad and generalized enjoyment of the outdoors that may take many forms over the years. Here's how to start off painlessly and avoid all the potential horrors just cited.

1. Familiarize youngsters *thoroughly* with the gun they will use, *before* going on the first hunt.

Take your youngster out in the field alone with the gun several times. Go through a thorough drill on loading and unloading and on how the safety mechanism works on that particular gun. Take some leisurely walks afield, and let the child carry the *unloaded* gun so that you can monitor how carefully it is handled. Correct a youngster anytime the gun is carelessly pointed the wrong way or anytime some other basic safety tenet is violated.

When youngsters have passed muster on carrying the empty

gun, let them load it for your next walks. Practice some informal target shooting or plinking to familiarize them with the sound and recoil of the gun. Convey to them that going on their first real small game hunt is a *privilege* they must *earn* by demonstrating that they are ready to hunt live game with a loaded gun. In a word, make them comfortable with the gun they'll be using. Give them a chance to test it thoroughly. If they don't like it, if it is too much gun for them, switch to a gun that is more comfortable for them or don't take them out until the following season. Make sure they are matched well enough to their firearm that they enjoy the excursion and don't regard it with dread as some necessary "duty" to be borne as stoically as possible.

2. *Acquaint the youngster with good gun-handling and safety-afield practices.* Review the basic Ten Commandments of Safety in Appendix III. Check with your local sporting-goods dealer to see if there are any mandatory or optional Hunter Safety courses being taught in the area for new hunters. If there are, be sure your youngster attends. These courses are usually well thought through and not the drudgery you may assume. In fact, they're a good idea for most adults!

Let your youngster discuss the safety considerations with you—don't just give lectures on the subject. To youngsters it may appear dumb to be so careful about an *un*loaded gun. Let them speak out on it and then explain why *any* gun should always be treated with maximum respect. Spending some time on safety (and courtesy!) afield before the hunt will make both your youngster and you far more comfortable when the big day finally dawns.

3. *Familiarize your youngster with the hunting regulations.* Be sure to explain all the legalities involved in small game hunting in your state and county. Remember: this is a privilege he or she is earning. Hunters of all ages should know the legal bag limits, when the hunting opens and closes each day, restrictions placed on shooting from near roads or buildings, restrictions about land access, and the other necessary rules and regulations governing your hunting.

You may be separated momentarily while afield. A young-ster should be thoroughly aware of what can and can't be done. Besides, it's good training for the child to do part of the work on the hunt and not be overly dependent on you or other adults. See that your youngster actually reads all the pertinent regulations. Don't just paraphrase them, as that way they are more easily forgotten. Again, if your youngster is well aware of exactly what is and isn't permissible afield, both of you will be far more com-fortable on the hunt.

4. *Choose the youngster's gun and ammunition with special care*. Small-sized youngsters need special consideration when it comes to guns and ammunition. *Don't* just casually hand them one of your guns and some shells without a second thought as to their smaller size, more muzzle-blast-sensitive ears and more recoil-tender shoulders.

The .22-caliber rifles are generally less of a problem than shotguns, since most of the former are lightweight and some-what scaled down in size when compared to a centerfire rifle or a shotgun. If possible, however, see that one of the lighter-model .22-caliber rifles is used. It will be easier to carry. Though shoul-der slings aren't normally found on .22-rimfire rifles, they make the gun much easier for a youngster to carry, since one can alternate carrying the gun over the shoulder with carrying it in the hand. This is especially important if the .22 is a bit bulkier and heavier because of a scope.

Shotguns can often be a significant problem for youngsters, especially if he or she is under 5 feet 3 inches tall and under 110 pounds. (They are also often a problem for small-framed women who don't do much shooting.) It is better to select a 20-gauge, 28-gauge or .410-caliber shotgun for the smaller youngster's use rather than the larger 12-gauge guns. The ammunition should be of the "low based" or standard-velocity type rather than the louder-barking, harder-kicking high-velocity loads. A recoil pad on the end of the shotgun is also a good idea.

Give particular consideration to providing the smallish young hunter with a smaller gun. The Winchester Model 37A "Youth" single-shot shotgun is one excellent, low-cost approach with its shorter, scaled-down gunstock that snugs properly into the shoulders of shorter-armed young hunters. Perhaps you could have the stock on an inexpensive shotgun cut down or at least shortened. When youngsters have to wrestle around awkwardly with a gunstock that is too heavy and too long, the apparent effects of recoil are magnified considerably because they can't snug the gun into the shoulder firmly yet comfortably and have their cheek well down and well forward on the butt stock as they should. A gun that is held too loosely without the cheek firmly anchored into the stock is going to kick far harder!

5. *Outfit the youngster with properly fitting and serviceable hunting clothes, not ill-fitting castoffs.* The young hunter should be clad comfortably in clothes that are designed for the job and fit properly. *You* wouldn't want to stumble around in a shirt or hunting coat that swallowed you up, constantly caught on brush and fences because it was so oversized, and generally made you look ridiculous. Neither does your youngster. Footwear should be comfortable (well broken in before the hunt!), of proper fit and adequately warm and waterproof for the terrain you'll be hunting. Oversized adult boots or undersized, improperly designed "play boots" that fit last year but not this year aren't a good idea. Painful blistered feet aren't any fun afield!

A suit of long underwear that fits, a good sturdy shirt and some briar-turning trousers will help round out the young hunter's wardrobe. If we can't afford, one way or another, to make our youngsters comfortable while they're hunting, we shouldn't have them out hunting to begin with.

6. *Plan special "youngster-balanced" hunts, especially the first time or two the child is afield.* This point can't be overemphasized. In most other shared activities, whether two-week vacations or merely a Saturday shopping excursion, some regard is given to the fact that a youngster or two will be along, and the trip is "balanced" a bit differently than might otherwise be the case. The same should certainly be true on a hunting trip, though, surprisingly enough, it usually isn't.

All too many adults just casually introduce the young person to hunting on an offhand, "let the kid come along on the next trip" basis. This in spite of the fact that youngsters, however much excited they may be at the beginning of the hunt, have a notoriously short attention span compared to most adults. Also, youngsters are shorter legged and can get tired or cold much easier than most adults. All these facts should be considered when introducing your child to small game hunting.

Plan the child's first hunt or two in areas where you have been particularly successful. Save these prime areas and don't shoot them out for yourself earlier in the season. Try to ensure as much action as possible so that the beginner has an enjoyable time and doesn't get bored.

Remember that children don't have a wealth of accumulated hunting memories and experiences to fall back on when the immediate hunt at hand is dragging. Your youngster doesn't have a *mature* appreciation of hunting and the outdoors with which to savor the smaller nuances of the experience and enjoy just being afield. The knowledge and capacity to appreciate fully all the aspects of the hunt must be acquired, just like so many other tastes, activities and pleasures that are still beyond a child's ken.

Make no mistake. Your youngster is there for *action*. The finer points come later. See that there is a fair share of that necessary excitement and action. Go to places you have hunted in past seasons and know well, to good places that usually yield game. Don't break in a new area or cover thin ground with the young hunter in tow. It won't work out.

Plan the hunt so that it isn't too strenuous. An arduous swamp country or steep-climbing country trip isn't usually a good idea. Plan to take several regularly spaced breaks during the hunt for rest and refreshment. You may not be getting hungry or tired, but chances are the youngster is.

Probably most important of all, *watch the youngster closely during the hunt*. Your frame of mind is all-important. You are not there primarily to hunt for yourself. You can do that on all the other trips without the child. You are there to see that he or she has a good hunt. Your own success is strictly secondary.

Steer youngsters toward the best coverts and spots. Let them have the first shot and the best shots; you wait and shoot only to keep game from escaping. Let them walk a bit in front of you so you can easily watch them (for safety's sake as well as for enjoyment) and steer them toward game they may not see or be ready for.

This is their hunt, not yours. Believe me, you'll experience far more satisfaction in seeing that they have a good hunt than by considering your own game bag. A child's excited, beaming face when downing a first rabbit or squirrel is better than any shot you could ever make yourself—a special moment for you to savor as you introduce the youngster to the whole wonderful world of the outdoors.

7. *See that the youngster knows a bit about the quarry.* Encourage the youngster to read up a bit on the game you will be after. This book is a start, but there are others, both of the hunting type and of the straight natural-history persuasion. Discuss your experiences and knowledge of the game. Get the youngster to *understand* what you are hunting and why you are hunting it in a specific fashion.

Knowledge makes the young hunter more competent in the field and provides extra enjoyment and interest. This single element helps lift hunting beyond the mere act of killing (which is mostly limited to the momentary excitement of the flush and the shot) to the level of a well-rounded appreciation of all aspects of the sport. The appreciation of the countryside, of the game, of the act and process of hunting—which far transcends the momentary adrenaline of the kill—all is built on the hunter's knowledge. And this knowledge should be acquired from books and from conversations with older hunters, to draw on their experiences and knowledge.

8. *Teach youngsters how to clean game and, except for an initial demonstration or two, see to it that they clean all their own game.* The hunt doesn't end with the kill. Good sportsmen utilize the tasty meat that they bring to bag, and hunters aren't competent unless they are cleaning and dressing their own game. There is extra satisfaction for the youngster in doing this alone, rather than being treated merely as a . . . child.

250

Probably the most important thing of all in introducing a young person to small game hunting is to *be patient*. Answer those "silly" questions fully and clearly. They aren't silly to children. Take the time to train them properly before the hunt. Spend the money to outfit them properly with gear and equipment. To keep the youngster's attention and interest, be flexible about how long you hunt and where and how. If boredom sets in, fold it up and go home. Don't exhaust the child and make the whole experience tedious by overdoing things. There's always another day. That's probably the way you started, and if you get exasperated, take some consolation from the fact that this youngster will probably be sharing that same exasperation and be thanking you with redoubled fervor about twenty years from now—in introducing your *grandchild* to the whole marvelous world of small game hunting and outdoor appreciation.

APPENDIX III

The Ten Commandments of Safety*

1. Treat every gun with the respect due a loaded gun.
2. Be sure of your target before you pull the trigger.
3. Always be sure that the barrel and action are clear of obstruction.
4. Never point your gun at anything you do not want to shoot.
5. Never leave your gun unattended unless you first unload it.
6. Avoid alcoholic beverages both before and after shooting.
7. Never climb a tree or cross a fence with a loaded gun.
8. Never shoot at a hard, flat surface or the surface of water. Make sure you always have a safe backstop.
9. Carry only empty guns, taken down or with the action open, into your camp, car or home.
10. Store guns and ammunition separately, beyond the reach of children.

(A postscript would be to wear shooting glasses at all times and, where desirable and practical, to utilize ear protection.)

*Reproduced courtesy of Winchester-Western division of Olin Industries.

Nutritional Value of Small Game

In this era of exploding health problems involving heart and circulatory diseases and other diet-related illnesses, people are becoming ever more conscious of what they eat. They want to know how fattening it is (the calorie count), how much fat it includes, how much food value it offers (the protein content, primarily), and maybe even what chemicals it contains. These are good and legitimate questions—especially as junk food seems to be increasing each year.

Not only is small game tasty fare if prepared properly (see chapters 14 and 15), it also offers excellent food values and is a particularly good choice for growing youngsters, who can put it to good use as they explode upward seemingly overnight.

Take rabbit, for example. A 100-gram serving (about 3½ ounces) of this most widely harvested small game animal, a serving containing only 135 calories before cooking, supplies 21 grams of protein but just 5 grams of fat, whereas the same amount of choice sirloin has 313 calories, only 16.9 grams of protein, and a whopping 26.7 grams of fat. For ham the figures are similar: 308 calories, 15.9 grams of protein, and 26.6 grams of fat; for pork, around 500 calories, only about 10 grams of protein, and more than 50 grams of fat! Even lean hamburger has twice the calories and four times the fat contained in the same amount of wild rabbit. And other game, small or large—squirrel or venison—is just as nutritious as rabbit. So enjoy this high-protein, low-fat meat often. It's good for you!